VOICES OVERHEARD

Biblical Characters that Speak

Randy L. Quinn

CSS Publishing Company
Lima, Ohio

VOICES OVERHEARD

FIRST EDITION
Copyright © 2023
by CSS Publishing Co., Inc.

Library of Congress Cataloging-in-Publication Data
Names: Quinn, Randy L., 1956- author.
Title: Voices overheard : biblical characters that speak / Randy L Quinn.
Description: Lima, Ohio : CSS Publishing Company, 2023.
Identifiers: LCCN 2022054117 (print) | LCCN 2022054118 (ebook) | ISBN
    9780788030765 (paperback) | ISBN 9780788030772 (adobe pdf)
Subjects: LCSH: Narrative preaching. | First person narrative. |
    Bible--Biography--Sermons.
Classification: LCC BV4235.S76 Q56 2023   (print) | LCC BV4235.S76
(ebook)
    | DDC 251--dc23/eng/20230130
LC record available at https://lccn.loc.gov/2022054117
LC ebook record available at https://lccn.loc.gov/2022054118

For more information about CSS Publishing Company resources, visit our website at www.csspub.com, email us at csr@csspub.com, or call (800) 241-4056.

e-book:
ISBN-13: 978-0-7880-3077-2
ISBN-10: 0-7880-3077-9

ISBN-13: 978-0-7880-3076-5
ISBN-10: 0-7880-3076-0   PRINTED IN USA

CONTENTS

To Ronda,
the only person who heard every voice in this book,
and usually endured the stress of wondering
if they would be heard the way I had hoped!
You are a saint!

FOREWORD

The first time I heard Randy preach I was a young associate pastor. As part of the United Methodist connectional system, Randy had just been appointed to the church where I was serving. Churches are always nervous about new pastors. Will this one fit in with us? Will they love us? Will they be awkward in the pulpit or eloquent? As the associate pastor, much of my role over the previous months had been to reassure people that all would be well.

That first Sunday, I have no idea what scripture Randy had preached on, but I do remember how I felt afterward. In speaking with my now-husband, Brian, about the service, I remember saying that I was impressed at how much I felt Randy had already connected with the congregation. Where some pastors may agonize over the perfect first sermon with a new congregation, perhaps trying to make some grand summation of the gospel, Randy unobtrusively let us, as hearers, into his life story. Instead of a pastor in a pulpit high above the congregation, Randy seemed like one of us. And the result was that his story illuminated our own stories. His story illuminated the good news and allowed it to be experienced by the congregation in a new way, a way that put us at ease and reassured us of God's presence in our lives.

Sermons should be that. They should be stories that invite us to see the work of God in our lives and in the lives of those around us. Too often sermons can feel like theological treatises or motivational speeches. Neither provokes the change of life required by the good news. People are changed not by arguments or persuasion but by authentic stories.

Randy's sermons are that, authentic. They draw us all into the sacred story of our faith. They make the characters of scripture come alive. In Randy's words, the people of the Bible move from mere literary figures, flat on the page, to real people whose lives were changed by an encounter with the divine. It is as if they were in the sanctuary sitting among us sharing their testimony. With Randy giving them voice, we can begin to see how the good news touches real lives. And then it occurs to us that it is not just our lives that God cares about, but it is also the people we encounter: the cashier at the grocery store, the grumpy neighbor, the quirky business owner, the skeptical teacher, the troubled teenager, the little boy on the playground, the overwhelmed young mother, the single dad. Everyone has a story to tell, if we just listen.

So listen in. Overhear the musings, the questions, the revelations, the excitement as these stories invite us into the encounter we all wish we could have: a moment with God.

Savor these stories. Allow them to speak to you like a conversation with a friend. With fresh eyes and ears, encounter the sacred through their eyes.

Brenda Kostner Johnson
December 2020

VOICES OF LIVES JESUS TOUCHED

I originally preached this series of sermons during Lent in 2008, including the "finale" of the series, an Easter sermon. At the time I was serving a "county seat" church in northeast Kansas, and I based the series on the gospel lessons in the Revised Common Lectionary, Cycle A. It is clear I took liberties with the story of each character, filling in where there is little evidence. Most of what is portrayed, however, is consistent with scriptural and historical records.

From my previous experience with "first person" sermons, I have learned there is no need to "dress" the part. Early in my ministry, I found small articles of clothing to denote the change in character, with things such as a different robe, holding a shepherd's crook, or donning a keffiyeh (an Arabic headscarf). I did not do so during this series. Typically, I read the text, then simply stepped outside the pulpit and began the sermon. The congregation quickly made the connection with the character and allowed me to be a different person — even when I took on the role of a woman!

I always made a manuscript available, including biblical references and footnotes. Not included in this collection are the bibliographies I used.

PAUL

I am Saul, of Tarsus, also known as Paul. I'm not really sure why your pastor invited me to speak today.

I mean, he explained his concept. He told me he wanted to invite people to speak to you during Lent, people whose lives had been touched by Jesus. But unlike the others he invited, I didn't meet Jesus until after his death and resurrection. In that sense, I'm more like you than I am the others he invited (1 Cor. 15:8).

Nor am I sure I have anything to say that you haven't already heard before. I mean, I wrote much of what you call the New Testament. You've all read my letters. You've heard Luke's account of my life. What more can I say?

That's when your pastor said he not only wanted me to tell my story, he wanted me to speak first because, well, because in his mind none of you would be here if it weren't for me. You see, while he believes the church was born on Pentecost, he is convinced it was only a branch of Judaism until I began to seriously evangelize Gentiles.

And while there is some truth to that suggestion, I guess the real problem I have with his invitation is the premise of his series of sermons. How will telling you my story help deepen your faith? My story is not what's important in worship; you see, I believe telling the story of Jesus should be the focus.

That's why I made it a point throughout my ministry to only speak about Christ (Rom. 15:18; 2 Cor. 4:5). And if anyone gives me credit for shaping the church, they have forgotten I was only acting as a vessel, a tool, an instrument of God (1 Cor. 3:8). I am not the one who founded the church; God did.

I know I often included my personal story in my preaching. I would tell people how my life was changed when I met Jesus. I'm sure you've heard that story before. How I was a committed leader among the Jews, a Pharisee among Pharisees (Phil. 3:5). And I took offense with the way the followers of Jesus were reinterpreting the scriptures — even though I hadn't even met the man. At the time I was proud to stand by as the first Christian was put to death for his faith (Acts 8:1). I became zealous in my attempts to round up all who called on Jesus, going as far as Damascus to find them (Acts 9:2).

I'm no longer proud of that era in my life. It's part of why I'm not sure your pastor invited me here today. I am the least qualified to be an apostle (1 Cor. 15:8). The word, apostle, by the way, means someone who is sent, an emissary.

Of course, it was on the road to Damascus that I met Jesus (Acts 9:5). And that's when my life began to change. And that is how I became an apostle (Rom. 1:1).

So ... well ... maybe ... I suppose it is not a far stretch to find myself sent here to speak to you, as an apostle to the Gentiles in all ages (Rom. 11:13).

Whenever I came to a new city, I always began in the synagogue on the Sabbath. I would share the story of our common faith from the time of Moses to David. I went on to explain how Jesus came as a descendant of

David to Israel. It was a hard thing for them to accept — as my own story suggests. But some would want to hear more, so we would find other times and places to meet. Eventually, we would leave the synagogue and form our own community of faith.

The church as you know it began in those times and places. Many of us would worship on the Sabbath with the Jews and then gather on the first day of the week with Christians and worship again. Our Sunday gatherings were often modelled on the only form of worship we had known. In fact, if you were to attend a Sabbath service today, you'd find many similarities remain between the church and the synagogue.

I was a stickler, however. I would not abide those who only went through the motions, who made a form of idolatry out of rituals and traditions. To me, the grace of God was being celebrated and it should always include a sense of joy and celebration, especially in light of the resurrection!

I'm sure you know what I mean.

During Lent, for example, I know some of you will likely participate in rituals of fasting. You might give up chocolate, for example. But when you make it a rule or a ritual, it loses its significance. Being righteous is more than fulfilling the expectations of Lent. Righteousness begins by accepting the grace that frees us from the rules and invites us to live in new ways.

Lent can help us remember what that means.

It's a fine line, though, a line that is easily transgressed.

Which is why I keep my focus on the death and resurrection of Jesus. If our lives do not reflect that story, then we have failed to be the church. We join him in our own death when we are baptized. We join our story with his, living out his purpose in us (Phil. 2:5, 13).

That is not to say that Lenten disciplines should be ignored. There is a role for taking vows as we recommit ourselves to God's authority (see Acts 21:26).

But like the Law of Moses, it is only a tool for us to see who we are, to recognize our need for grace, not a means of earning God's favor.

It's funny, really.

When I met Jesus, I was struck down. I was blind. I was on my knees. I was responding to a voice I didn't recognize. As I said, I was blind, so I couldn't see who was speaking. So, I asked who he was. After telling me he was Jesus, he began to tell me what to do (Acts 9:6).

I'm only glad he didn't give me a detailed list that day! I might have chosen to remain blind!

I mean, really? Who would choose to be imprisoned or stoned or shipwrecked or chased out of town — more than once!? I was not only content with my role in society, I was also a respected scholar. Why would I want to leave that?

Jesus only told me the next step. And then the next step. One step at a time for the rest of my life.

After three days, I received my sight. Then I began to tell the story of Jesus (Acts 9:20). I had been trained in the arts of rhetoric and debate and I used those tools to convince others about the truth of Jesus. I also spent time learning from those who had known Jesus and began formulating arguments, arguments that would eventually become known as apologetics. In formulating those arguments, I often found myself wrestling with the deepest truths of God's nature and God's grace.

By the time I wrote the letter to the Romans, some of which you heard read earlier, I had a fairly coherent concept of who Jesus was. I knew how he fit within the framework of Judaism, as well as the role of the Law and the primacy of grace.

One of the key things I learned was that righteousness is not earned but granted (Rom. 5:17; 8:30). It is a free gift. And nothing in this life — or the next — can separate us from the love of God (Rom. 8:38).

I never would have realized that had I not met Jesus. Knowing that has changed the way I see myself and the world around me. I am a beloved — and forgiven — child of God. And so are you.

Thanks be to God. Amen.

John 3:1-17

NICODEMUS

Hi, my name is Nicodemus. You can call me Nick if you'd like. Your pastor tapped me on the shoulder and asked me to tell you what it was like to meet Jesus, to have my life touched by his presence, his power, his grace.

I hesitated to come at first. I suppose that's always been my style. I prefer to stay in the background. I prefer to listen more than I speak. In fact, from my youth I was taught that it was better to remain silent and be thought a fool than to open my mouth and remove all doubt.

What the proverb actually says is "Fools who keep quiet are deemed wise; those who shut their lips are smart" (Pr. 17:28).

The truth is I was an important part of my faith community and was recognized as a man of wisdom — and not just because of my silence. I not only knew the Bible and was clear about what it means, I also lived a life of faith that was often lifted up as an example for others to emulate.

People frequently asked my opinions about the scriptures and about how to live our lives in response to them.

But I was more comfortable being in the background than being in the limelight. I preferred to listen and whisper my thoughts rather than proclaim them in public settings. For that reason, I suppose, I was never considered for any of the chief positions in the Sanhedrin or among the circles of Pharisees (Jn. 7:50).

That's also why I first met Jesus the way I did (Jn. 3:1-2).

I had heard of Jesus. (Who hadn't?) Then I overheard some of his stories and parables. And I wondered. And, I admit now, I was worried.

What if Jesus was right?
What if I had spent my whole life looking for faith in the wrong place?
What if I had invested myself in some-thing that was doomed to fail?

I didn't want to be like the man who was arguing with his wife on vacation. She had looked at the map and insisted he was going the wrong direction. But he was making such good time he didn't want to turn around.

I didn't want to make good time going toward the wrong destination — but I was also afraid of making a course correction. I was actually paralyzed by the dilemma. I'm not sure you can imagine what it would have been like. It would be more than a little embarrassing. I was a leading Pharisee who had doubts — doubts about my faith, doubts about my wisdom, doubts about . . . well . . .

. . . maybe you can understand it if I told you I felt like someone who had been a campaign staffer for Donald Trump who wondered if Elizabeth Warren was the best candidate after all.

If Jesus were right, I would need to make a radical change in my life — and just the thought of that terrified me!

But as frightening as the possibilities seemed, I decided to meet Jesus, although I insisted we meet privately. Face to face. Well, it was dark, so it wasn't really "face to face" in the sense that I could see him very well. But you know what I mean.

I realized how nervous I was when I became sarcastic in my responses. "How in the world can I re-enter my own mother's womb?" I asked. Knowing my mother had died several years earlier made my words seem even more accusatory than I might have meant to sound — had I been clear headed. It was my emotional anxiety that came through — my fears, my worries, my embarrassments.

For all of that, Jesus impressed me as a man who never lost sight of his purpose. He not only knew who he was, he also knew who I was. In the darkness, I heard a warm smile in his voice; I also felt the increasing rate of my heart as he spoke.

I left that night more convinced that he was right and at the same time more paralyzed. I couldn't find a way to turn. Whatever I did from that moment on would mean a betrayal — either a betrayal of the truth I had been exposed to or a betrayal of my past and my reputation.

Although Jesus was right, to do more than to acknowledge that intellectually, I had to change the way I lived, the way I spoke; I would have to affiliate with different people and leave behind the status and role I had earned over the years. I was frightened as well as embarrassed.

For a while, I tried to keep up the appearances of a leading Pharisee while inwardly hoping the truth of Jesus would be revealed and I would be safe acknowledging what I had decided. But instead the tensions rose and it became harder to stand in the middle.

One time I betrayed my position — and almost lost my credibility among the Jews. I tried to plead for a proper hearing for Jesus, thinking that if I spoke about the *process* rather than the *issue* I might make a difference for Jesus while remaining in the background (Jn. 7:50-51).

But that comment placed me in the spotlight. Everything I said or did after that day was suspect. And I became less vocal than I had ever been before.

Finally, I could no longer remain silent. Jesus had been crucified and I realized I failed to use my influence to protect him. I stood up as a follower of Jesus and asked if I could assist with his burial (Jn. 19:38-40). It may have been too little too late, but I could no longer remain in the shadows. (I also found I was not alone. Another leading Pharisee, Joseph, became my public ally as we provided a proper burial for the one we had come to believe bore witness to the truth of God's love and grace.)

That was both the end of our troubles and the beginning of our troubles. We were no longer welcome among the leading citizens of Jerusalem because of our actions. At the same time we were held under suspicion by the followers of Jesus because of our past.

My reticence for which I had become well known, and by which I had gained a favorable reputation, became the source of my vulnerability and weakness.

Eventually, I was welcomed by the church — but only after many years of silence — and maybe would not have been welcomed at all had it not been for people like Barnabas who introduced several Pharisees to the church council — including a man who became known as Paul (Acts 9:27).

But even without Barnabas, my life would never be the same. I had met Jesus. He was no longer a person I talked about or heard about. And unlike so many people I've known, he had listened without issuing a judgment about me, offering instead his vision of God's unlimited grace, and the possibility that I could be given a second chance at life.

My life would never be the same after that encounter.

You all remember the famous words Jesus said to me? "For God so loved the world that he gave his only Son, so that everyone who believes in him may not perish but may have eternal life" (Jn. 3:16). The words I remember best are what he said next, "Indeed, God did not send the Son into the world to condemn the world, but in order that the world might be saved through him" (Jn. 3:17).

I was not condemned for being wrong; I was simply offered a gift. And while I was reluctant at first, I eventually accepted it — and my life has never been the same.

Thanks be to God.

Amen.

THE SAMARITAN WOMAN

Hi. I was *so excited* when your pastor asked me to talk to you today! I was especially excited when I learned that you live in a small town — just like my hometown of Sychar.

So, you probably understand some of what happened to me. I was in my mid-forties. I had already been through five bad marriages, and well, it was hard enough to find a man who wanted to spend time with me so I didn't pressure the sixth one into marriage. I'll bet anyone in your town with a similar story would have had a hard time coming to church. In fact, I suspect most of you would have talked about her behind her back — or maybe even to her face!

(Some people actually did that to me, by the way. One woman actually told me, "You've made your bed, now you can sleep in it"!)

People were so cruel to me — it was not only the way they spoke to me, it was also the way they looked at me and the way they spoke *about* me. I began to shut myself into the house most of the time. I went to the well in the middle of the day, for instance, rather than joining the women in their daily conversations.

Don't tell me you don't know about those. You meet for coffee and you talk about all of the people you know — who's in the hospital, whose granddaughter is getting married, and the weather. (I think the men gather and talk about the same kinds of things only they say they're 'solving the world's problems' because they can't solve their own!)

I don't get into that stuff.

Actually, I wished I could be included; but my life was a mess and no one had kind words to say to me. No one wanted to be around me. No one wanted their daughter to be like me, so they avoided me as much as I avoided them. If I had a daughter, I might have introduced her to that social setting, but I had no children and no friends. So instead I shut myself off from the world and tried to mind my own business.

I didn't like who I had become and neither did anyone else. Except for the fact that I gave everyone else someone to talk about, no one really seemed to care about my plight, either. And no one, not even my current boyfriend, made any attempt to treat me with respect. I had long ago forgotten what love really looked like.

That all changed one spring day. Unlike today, it was sunny and warm. Warm enough that most people sought out shady places to sit.

I went to the well at my usual time, and there by the well was a stranger — I knew he wasn't from around here. (You can just tell, can't you?) But usually the only men I met at the well used worn-out pick-up lines, and I was in no mood for a new relationship. So I tried to ignore him.

But he couldn't be ignored.

It wasn't what he said, really. It was the way he spoke to me. He spoke about the same things my neighbors spoke about — my past, my present, my future — but instead of naming it all with disdain, he named it with compassion. He knew I had made poor choices in life, but amazingly he didn't make me feel bad for making them.

Even when he asked me to give him a drink of water, he asked in such a way that I felt honored to assist him. I couldn't remember ever being asked to do something that didn't feel like I was the servant whose only allowed response was, "yes, sir."

He saw inside me — and somehow his eyes saw something loveable.

Now, I admit, it was so different from the conversation I had anticipated that I kept trying to change the subject. His kindness kept putting me off balance — no one had ever treated me that way before. He kept his ears open to my soul while I kept trying to use my own bitterness as a barrier between us. (I'm not sure I was really aware I was doing that, but as I listened to the story being read to you again this morning, I could really hear it — with some embarrassment, I might add.)

I listened for any opportunity to make him think less of me. In my mind I was unlovable. He was a Jew; I was a Samaritan; so I tried to use that difference to give him a reason to treat me with contempt. But it wouldn't work. I tried to use some of the theological arguments of our day to get him to take sides — so I could be on the other side. But no matter what I said, he continued to treat me with the utmost respect and dignity. He kept speaking and acting as if I was lovable!

You know, the scriptures never tell you my name. For much of my life, I felt like my name should have been "Mara," the name Naomi claimed after her sons and husband died (Ruth 1:20). Like her, bitterness was all I knew.

That all changed when I met Jesus.

I began to love myself and the people around me. My self-worth became evident and others no longer treated me with scorn. In fact, the Christians would later refer to me as "Photini," a name that means equal to the Apostles.

I became so concerned about the people in my own town that I went and told others about the man I had met — a man who changed my life. Later, he would actually *give* his life for us, but that day, it was the way he loved me that changed me.

That love took root and lived in me. It changed how I saw others and helped them see me in a new light. His loved changed me and his love changed our small town, too.

I am convinced that same love can take root in you, as well. In God's eyes, you are all lovable.

Thanks be to God.

Amen.

A Man Born Blind

Hi. Um. I'm not really sure why your pastor asked me to speak to you today. I mean, I'm not very comfortable talking about what happened to me. I guess I was that way from the very beginning — when people started blaming me for my blindness or blaming me for pretending I was blind. I'm not really sure why they blamed me, but they did. I think most people who asked me about it were only trying to find assurance that *they* were not to blame. In fact, most people who ask me to talk about it are more concerned with their own stories than mine.

So I've never been very comfortable talking about it.

But the truth is Jesus changed my life.

Before I met him, I didn't know there was anything different. I was born blind, so I didn't know there was a difference in color between a carrot and a pea; I only knew they tasted different and had different textures. I didn't know roses had colorful blossoms as well as delightful smells and prickly thorns. I didn't know how to tell the difference between a robin and a finch except by hearing their songs.

When I was born, my parents began to blame themselves. They thought they had done something wrong — and I was their punishment. I didn't know that some children were born truly loved. I didn't know that some children were loved so much that other parents adopted them.

I only knew I was a burden. I was a living reminder of whatever sin was in their past — a sin they never confessed to me, but a sin for which they spent most of their lives atoning.

In an effort to help them, I begged for money, and some days I did pretty well, but my parents never seemed to get over the scar my life left on their lives.

Don't get me wrong. If you asked, they would say they loved me. And I knew they did, but the kind of love they had for me was perfunctory. They fed me, they clothed me, they protected me; they provided the basic necessities of life — although it often felt as though they only did it so people couldn't accuse them of murder should something happen to me. They loved me in the way they cared for me, but I never got the sense that they cared *about* me.

Their love reminded me of the vast majority of people who put money in my bowl when I was begging: they felt sorry for me. They looked at me as if I were less than human.

It's funny, in some ways. Some people knew I couldn't see, so they would yell at me — as if I were also deaf! What they apparently didn't understand was that I relied upon my hearing in ways they didn't. I could hear things in the tone of voice that betrayed the truth of their lies. I could also hear things in the voices of people that told about their own sorrows, their own joys, and even the occasional voice of someone who genuinely cared about me.

Day after day, my parents would help me find a place to beg. And day after day, they would come back and take me home. I probably could have found my own way home, but I allowed them to do so — it gave them more to complain about, and that seemed to be their only purpose in life.

The truth is people never treated me as a human being. I was rarely spoken to; most people spoke about me instead. I was an obstacle for them to step over or around — in fact my parents placed me in the busiest intersections so more people would stumble over me — and then out of guilt they would place more money in my bowl.

Their alms were expressions of their guilt, you see. They were not given out of compassion for me.

I began to see that so clearly. I, who was blind, could see something they never saw. I began to feel sorry for the people who could see! Can you imagine that?

And then one day, a man came by. His voice was authoritative. People cleared the way in front of him. I thought at first he must be a high ranking Roman official as he approached — but his feet were quiet. He wasn't wearing any warrior boots.

Then he stopped as others spoke about me. It was the same kind of things I'd heard people whisper before. These people, people I'd never met, spoke as if I were not even present. "Who sinned," they asked, "this man or his parents?"

Now, if the man they asked could answer that question, I was all ears! I had wondered that, too. (Not that I could think of any sin I had committed; but I also found it hard to believe that the whole purpose for my life was to punish my parents.)

I'll never forget his words. Nor will I forget the warmth of his voice. "Neither sinned," he said. Then he spit on the ground. I felt the warm, wet, gritty mud on my eyes. And when he directed me to go and wash off, I got up and immediately did as I was told. (As

I said, he spoke with authority, so I did what he told me to do.)

But you can't imagine my surprise when the mud was gone!

I could see.

I didn't know exactly what I was looking at, but my eyes were able to see!

When I came back to the place where it began, there were familiar voices around me. It was almost as if I could hear their thoughts as well as their spoken words — either that or they were thinking out loud as if I were no longer blind but deaf instead! "Is this the same man?" they asked. (Only one asked me if I was the same person . . . and I only recognized him as he was walking away — I knew the sound of his walk and knew he was one of the most generous of all the almsgivers.)

But I never saw the man who spit on the ground and sent me off. So, I couldn't tell others who he was. Nor could I thank him.

Although, I did wonder if thanks was the appropriate response.

You see, instead of being blamed for being blind, I was now being blamed for being healed. Now I was being charged as a fraud. Even my own parents couldn't find relief from my newfound sight. They were examined and accused of fraud, too.

I became even more convinced it never was about their sin or mine. It was everyone else's. We had become the community scapegoats. Everyone's guilt was placed on our shoulders — and now they had to face their own sin because they could no longer find fault with us!

That made our lives more difficult. My parents wanted to disown me — as if the punishment they had been paying for all 27 years of my life were a tragic mistake. They were free from me, and it seemed as though they intended to keep it that way.

Finally a man with a familiar voice asked about my story. It turns out he was the same man who had healed me. Jesus.

All my life I had depended upon other people for the basic necessities of life. It was really good training for my spiritual awakening that happened the second time I met Jesus. I knew what many others didn't know — I knew how to depend on someone else. And every day I still depend upon God to take me places; I depend upon God to provide food for my table and clothing for my back. I depend upon God for the roof over my head as well as the words to speak.

I learned to depend upon others while I was blind.

Now I depend upon God. (And by the way, God is more dependable.)

I no longer beg for a living, and even though my parents rarely speak to me, I went to my father's trade of shearing sheep. And every time I hold a lamb in my arms, I remember that the Lord is my shepherd.

Thanks be to God.

Amen.

LAZARUS

Hi. My name is Lazarus. It's not a very common name anymore, but it was pretty common in my day. It was as common as "Larry" is to you, I suppose. In fact, you can call me "Larry" if you'd like.

How many of you have heard of me before?

Sometimes people confuse me with the story Jesus told about a man named Lazarus (Lk. 16:19-31). He was the one who begged for food outside the gates of a rich man when he was alive and was fed sumptuously at the bosom of Abraham when he died. How many of you remember that story?

Well, that wasn't me. It was another guy who had the same name — although he may have been imaginary. I think Jesus actually made up that story to make a point.

And while I wasn't as well off as some people were, neither was I a beggar like that Lazarus was — whether he was real or not. In fact, I owned my own home. My sisters and I opened our home to Jesus when he had some of his meetings. Maybe you know about my sisters, Mary and Martha?

You probably remember one part of one of those visits (Lk. 10:38-42). It was mealtime, and Martha was busy trying to get food on the table. She became upset with Mary who was listening intently to what Jesus had to say. It was one of those delightful times when Jesus was telling stories, stories that invited everyone to listen — men, women, and even children. I think it was our laughter that made Martha realize what she was missing.

Jesus came to our house so often that I thought of him like a brother. We shared stories together. We shared jokes together. We shared secrets with each other. My sisters and I always welcomed his presence, and he genuinely seemed to enjoy our company as well. I suppose that made us special in his eyes — and maybe unique among our peers.

But what happened to me was unlike anything anyone else had ever experienced. I mean, I know there were other people who died and were then raised from the dead. I know Elijah raised a boy from the dead, for instance, and Jesus brought a girl back from the dead (1 Kgs. 17:22, Lk. 8:54). But neither of them had been wrapped in burial cloths and placed in a tomb. None of the others, in fact, had been dead for more than a few hours.

I was in the *grave* for four days!

Believe me, I know (even though I don't remember much about those four days). I'm only glad I'm not claustrophobic!

What I remember was being sick. So sick that we asked Jesus to come and be with us. He probably could have made me well — I mean he healed people of far worse ailments. But Jesus didn't get there in time.

And while my sisters held it against him that he didn't come, I didn't. I knew that his mere presence was creating a stir with the officials. The last time he had been there they had threatened to have him put to death (Jn. 11:8). So it was fine with me if he didn't come and see me.

I was so sick, it took all the energy I had to sit up and open my eyes. I was deathly sick; but still I knew that his life was far more important than mine.

So, I went to lie down, and I went to sleep.

(Apparently I died in my sleep. My breathing stopped, anyway. So did my heart. My sisters tell me there was no response to any of their attempts to raise me — and then my body grew cold and stiff. My funeral was planned and I was buried in our family tomb just outside of town.)

I honestly don't remember that part. (I've wondered what my friends said about me — all I know for sure was Jesus didn't come to the funeral. I've also heard how Jesus wept outside my tomb.) What most people want to know is what heaven was like — but I don't remember. I wish I did, but I don't.

They tell me that Mary and Martha were both a little upset with Jesus when he finally arrived. Well, maybe more than a little upset.

I wasn't there, so I can't be sure. All I remember was Jesus calling my name. I sat up, but I couldn't open my eyes. They were wrapped in some kind of cloth. And when I went to pull off the cloth, I realized my hands were tied to my sides.

It was like one of those dreadful nightmares. I couldn't move. I couldn't speak. I couldn't see. But I could still hear Jesus calling. I worked hard to get on my feet and walk toward the sound of his voice — although it was more like a hop than a walk.

It wasn't until someone unwrapped me that I realized what was going on.

I had been in a tomb! A story like Edgar Allen Poe might tell — except I don't remember the anxiety, the worry, the fear of being in the tomb. I only know the joy of finding new life.

Some people turn over new pages in their lives when they finish their course of study. Some people begin a new phase in their lives when they marry off their last child. Some people experience similar kinds of new adventures when a child is born or a new job is begun.

Like them, I had been given a chance to live differently.

Even my sisters were changed. They no longer spoke about believing what Jesus said. They began to live their lives differently. They were no longer interested in having the right answers, but were always looking for the right questions.

But a part of my new life was living with guilt. You see, the Jewish leaders responded to my new life by making plans to put Jesus in his own tomb (Jn. 11:46-53). He chose not to come and see me while I was sick in order to save his life — and now he would lose his life because he gave me new life.

I thought his life was of more value than mine; turns out he thought my life was of more value than his.

And that's part of why I'm telling you the story. You see, I think Jesus thinks that about your life, too. I think he sees so much hope and promise in what you can do that he is willing to lay down his life so you can experience it — and share it.

You may not realize it, but you have been raised from the dead, too. You have been given a new chance to live.

Thanks be to God.

Amen.

PILATE

Some people want to blame me for what happened. Me. Pontius Pilate. It wouldn't surprise me if you do, too. And while I take full responsibility for what I did, I'm not sure "blame" is the proper word. Maybe "credit" is a better description. I saved the Roman Empire. I should be considered a hero.

But let me explain myself before you make your judgments about me.

Let me first go back several years. Unlike most of the other governors throughout the Roman Empire, I had earned my right to govern. Most of the others had inherited their right to rule.

And unlike me, they were wimps who were afraid to make decisions that might anger people. There were some who were political appointees, but those were the ones who were afraid to offend people — whether they were superiors or subordinates. All of them were afraid to make decisions; but every leader eventually learns that not making a decision is making a decision — and usually it's the wrong one.

Me, on the other hand, I had worked my way up through the ranks. I began as a foot soldier in the Roman Army. And I learned early in my career that you could get promoted and advance through the ranks if you weren't afraid to make decisions. So I decided as a young soldier that I was going to make them. And, as anyone who has ever been in a leadership position knows, some decisions are not popular. Some are actually wrong. But I learned from my mistakes and I soldiered on. And if you'll take the time to look, you'll see that overall my record was good.

I made hard decisions. I made good decisions. In fact, the only time I ever remember going back on a decision I made was when I placed those images of Caesar in the Jewish temple courtyards. I knew it would upset them, but I thought it was important for them to know that it was our emperor who gave them permission to worship their God — not the other way around.

I was going to enforce the decision I made with the sword, in fact. I had soldiers lined up and ready to execute any rebel who objected. But hundreds of Jewish citizens simply prostrated themselves on the ground and opened their necks to the soldier's swords. I didn't know it was possible to willingly die for what you believed — but clearly they did.

In the end, I decided their blood wasn't worth cleaning up, so I withdrew the soldiers and then removed the images.

That was an exception, however. You see, it was my willingness to make decisions and to stand by them that was noticed by my superiors, and eventually by the ruling class in Rome. So I was given the role of leading the Jewish people — a people that were surely going to cause problems for Caesar if I didn't make wise decisions.

I had earned my right to rule, and I knew I would do a good job.

Admittedly, I didn't know much about their religion — although honestly I didn't know much about my own, either. I was what you might call a "pragmatic deist." I believed in God when it suited me — when I thought it was worth believing in God. But my life didn't revolve around any gods; rather the gods were simply called upon to help me accomplish my goals. Sometimes I even called on them for political reasons. As far as I was concerned, any divine beings could be called on when I needed them — they didn't call on me and they had no rights to claim my allegiance, either.

One time, I took money from the Jewish temple funds and created a water viaduct for my palace. (Those poor naïve fools who put money in their offering plates had no idea how it was being used anyway.) When they found out about it, though, some people were offended. But that time I didn't change my mind. I stuck with my decision.

I had the soldiers slaughter anyone who objected. Hundreds fled that day, but I think several hundred also died. Their God couldn't protect them — nor could their God tell me how to run my office.

Some people called me ruthless. I preferred to think of it as decisive.

Curiously, my pragmatic approach to religion didn't seem to bother the Jewish leaders — all of whom liked to wrap themselves in their religion as if it made them better than me or more powerful than Rome. Sometimes I wondered if they were just as pragmatic about their faith as I was!

What we had was a great relationship, though. There were times when I was able to use their religion to make decisions that weren't popular so it looked like they were the ones to blame; and there were times when

I could support them by making decisions they didn't want to make so they could maintain their prestige.

Take the story of your Jesus, for example.

As far as I was concerned, he was a nobody. And I would have had no problem sending him to prison or having him beheaded like Herod did to John. (By the way, that was one of the few examples of someone who inherited the throne that wasn't afraid to make a decision — and I have to admit I respected him for that.)

But the Jews wanted to pin the blame on me so they could look innocent. They were trying to play me — a man who knew how to see through them. So I used their passions against them and made it look like their problem and their decision instead of mine. I had the best of both worlds! I made a decision that made perfect sense from the perspective of Rome — and I got to pin it on the Jewish leaders!

If you ask me, it was brilliant!

If it weren't for my wife's concerns for the victim, however, I probably wouldn't even have noticed him. (I never did understand what it was about this Jesus that so enthralled her — but she was convinced he had something to offer both the Jews and the Romans.) Me, on the other hand, I couldn't tell the difference between him and the dozens of other trouble-makers who came pleading their cases before me.

In many ways, he reminded me of the people who were willing to lay down their lives to keep Caesar's image out of the temple. He didn't object. It made me wonder if *I* was the one being played rather than me playing the Jewish leaders! (And I'll admit it could have been the second time I changed my mind if more people had offered to substitute their lives for his — or to offer their lives as a part of the cost of taking his life.)

But it was a fleeting thought. No one came to his defense, no one was willing to lay down their life for his and I knew what I had to do. This man was trying to usurp the power of Rome by claiming to be a king. I needed to put him away.

Fortunately, the Jewish leaders gave me a way to make it look like I was innocent when I condemned him. In fact, I made a great theater out of it. I washed my hands in a public venue — and was able to hide my disdain for this man and the people who opposed the Roman Emperor.

I made lots of decisions like that. Unfortunately, one of those decisions caused another regional governor to become alarmed. He was more politically connected than I was, and so after ruling in Jerusalem for a brief ten years, I was removed from office.

It really was unfair. I should have been considered a hero for saving Rome. Instead I had to live the final years of my life in seclusion. And it wasn't long after I left that the Jews revolted — a conflict that ended when the Roman soldiers destroyed their temple.

I still think I did the right thing for the right reason. It accomplished what I had hoped to accomplish — and being the pragmatist I was, I count that as a success.

And unless you can find people willing to die for him, I have no doubt that I'd do it again.

Acts 10:34-43
John 20:1-18

PETER

I was so glad when your pastor asked me to come today. I couldn't wait to tell you that Jesus is alive and that I'm forgiven!

Now you may not think that's so significant, but I do. I mean the forgiven part. The fact that Jesus was alive was something we had been told but didn't understand. We had seen Lazarus come out of the tomb, so we weren't as surprised by the resurrection as you might guess. But the forgiveness, that was more than I could comprehend — almost more than I can comprehend still.

I remember when Jesus first called me to be one of his followers (Mt. 4:18-19). I had been a fisherman. I worked with my brother Andrew, in company with the Zebedees, with James and John and their father.

With our two boats, we were on the water every morning, and almost every evening, too. It was hard work, but it was rewarding work. We got to spend time with our family; we got to spend time enjoying the sunshine on sunny days. We spent many of our hours telling stories and laughing together.

We even played tricks on each other. Once I pretended to bring a huge fish into the boat. When

Andrew saw me struggling, he wasn't sure what to do — but when I pretended to bring the huge fish into the boat, he was so startled that he fell overboard!

There were hard days, too; days when there were no fish to be caught and our nets were empty (Lk. 5:5; Jn. 21:3). Some of those days were spent mending nets. But for the most part, it was enjoyable work.

But then along came Jesus. He simply called to us — and the tender authority with which he spoke seemed to leave us no choice but to leave our boats, our nets, to leave our families behind. We simply walked off the job as we began to follow Jesus.

And while I tried fishing again, it was never the same. Jesus had changed my life with his teachings; he even suggested that my name be changed from Simon — a name that had to do with my facial features — to Peter — a name that had to do with my personality (Mt. 16:18). I went from being flat-nosed (which is what Simon means) although some of my friends thought of it as hard-nosed, to being a rock (which is what Peter means), someone on whom you could depend.

And that's what I tried to be, dependable. I was always there with Jesus. I was like his right-hand man. And I thought he was depending on me.

It turns out I was depending upon him far more than I realized until that Passover weekend when he died and was buried. He was only in the tomb three days — actually part of three different days — but they seemed like an eternity as I remembered all the ways he had met my needs — all of the times he had been my rock and how rarely I had been someone on whom he could depend.

I mean, he healed my mother-in-law when she was sick (Mt. 8:14-15). And when I stupidly stepped out of a boat onto the water, he saved me from nearly drowning (Mt. 14:30-31)! He calmed the waters when we thought we were going to drown (Mt. 8:26); and more than once he made sure we had enough to eat — me and thousands of others (Mt. 14:20)!

I had only really known him for about three years but it seemed like he had always been there. He was always dependable.

But when things became difficult for him . . . I tried to blend into the crowd. I became like one of the cobblestones. I kept silent when I should have spoken. I disappeared when he needed me most. I made a promise to be with him on Thursday — but I broke my promise before the night was over (Mt. 26:75).

Amazingly, he forgave me. He reinstated me. He had told us that we should be willing to forgive those who sinned against us seventy times seventy times (Mt. 18:22). He had told parables about the way God forgives the multitudes of our sin (Lk. 7:41).

But I was still surprised when he actually practiced what he preached and forgave me! He made sure I knew I had been forgiven when he asked me three different times if I loved him — and three different times he told me what I was to do (Jn. 21:15-17).

Then on Pentecost of that same year, he gave me his Holy Spirit so that I was able to preach and proclaim the truth that I had been forgiven (Acts 2:14ff).

So, as I said, the fact that I was forgiven was more amazing to me than his being raised from the dead. But not only that, not only have I been forgiven, you've been forgiven, too!

I had a hard time realizing that, you know. At first I thought Jesus was only talking about the Jews when he gave me the "keys to the kingdom," when he gave me the authority to offer forgiveness (Mt. 16:19). I thought when he told us to tell everyone about his love and his salvation — to go to Jerusalem and Judea and Samaria and to the ends of the earth — I thought he meant to the Jews who lived in those places (Acts 1:8).

Boy was I in for a surprise!

I was ready to limit what God was doing — and then I had a vision that made me listen to some Gentiles (Acts 10:9-16). I wound up in the home of Cornelius — a man who became my friend and colleague. It was while I was there, like a light bulb going off, I knew that God's love was not limited to just the Jews. It wasn't limited to people whose parents already knew about God. It was for everyone, including all of you.

It was like experiencing Easter all over again. There was the same mixture of confusion over what was taking place, the uncertainty about what God was doing, and then the crystal clear realization that God's forgiveness was meant for Cornelius and his family as much as it was meant for me and mine.

I could go on and on. But maybe the best way to conclude my comments today is to invite you to listen in on the "sermon" I preached when I was at the house of Cornelius, the first Gentile to became my friend. It's much like most of the sermons I preached in those early days of my ministry.

Hear now, from the 10th chapter of Acts.

VOICES AT THE FOOT OF THE CROSS

This series of sermons has a "story" behind it. The choir director at the church I was serving had repeatedly brought out an Easter Cantata at choir rehearsals early in January and then consistently set it aside. The cantata was *We Were There: A Dramatic Choral Experience for Easter* by Pepper Choplin (GlorySound, 2005). It features songs to complement the stories of people who were at the foot of the cross.

When pushed, the choir director would say we didn't have time to work on all the songs. Or she would make excuses about who would be gone on whatever date she would schedule the cantata. So, I made a proposal. I suggested that instead of doing the cantata as a whole piece, we could work on one song each week during Lent, and that I would complement the anthem with a sermon based on that week's character. She agreed and the plan was launched.

I began to formulate the characters as being told from the "first person" perspective. Two of the sermons were about women, however (Mary Magdalene and Mary, the mother of Jesus). I chose to not make those "first person" sermons. When Palm Sunday arrived, I suggested we could do the entire presentation, since the choir knew most of the songs already.

Listed here are the first-person sermons I preached during that series, as well as one other I think fits the genre. As is the case with the other sermons in this book, I took liberties with the characters, working within a framework I call "plausible fiction," knowing not everything can be verified.

JOHN

My name is John, sometimes known as the "disciple whom Jesus loved." I am an old man now, much older than I ever thought I'd become, but I still cherish the idea that I am loved and beloved. Jesus implied once that I might live until he returns, but the joy in my life comes from knowing that his love for me continues whether he returns in my lifetime or not (Jn. 21:22-23).

I still remember my first encounter with Jesus (Mk. 1:19-20). He had been preaching in and around our village, healing people and making quite an impression. My father had planted seeds of skepticism, though. "Isn't he a carpenter?" he would ask. "Shouldn't he be caring for his widowed mother instead of wandering around from town to town? Doesn't he know the commandment says to honor your mother and father?"

What my father meant was he believed we are to care for our parents in their old age, not abandon them. To him, Jesus had abandoned his own mother, and no one who would do that should be given the time of day.

His name was Zebedee, a name that means thunder. And when my father spoke, you could almost hear the thunder in his voice. So you might understand why I didn't tell him that I had gone to hear Jesus preach. There was something compelling about him. Jesus not only spoke with authority, but he seemed to have his heart in it — not like the others we had heard speak and preach (see Mt. 7:28-29). So when he called out to me that day on the beach, I simply got up and followed him (Mt. 4:21-22).

There were times when I felt the weight of my father's words, thinking that he probably thought I had abandoned him. But like Jacob leaving Isaac to find a wife or David leaving Jesse to serve Saul, I knew that God would provide for my father, just as I knew my own needs would be met.

After Jesus died, I tried to go fishing again (Jn. 21:2-3). We all did. But our hearts weren't in it. We had been changed by our time with Jesus. And when he met us on the shores of the lake that morning, we knew we had no choice but to leave our nets again, this time permanently (Jn. 21:4 ff). Fortunately, my father understood by then and gave us his blessing.

I'm not sure when or how, but early in our time together I realized Jesus and I were more like best friends than we were "teacher and student" or "master and disciple." I could see him grooming Peter to become the leader, but he shared things with me in confidence that the others never heard. I never begrudged the role Peter was given — in fact, most of the time I was glad he was the one making decisions, not me! Peter was meant to be the leader of the Disciples and the early church.

But I was the disciple whom Jesus loved. Our hearts were as one.

So, when we stood at the foot of the cross, I was not surprised that he asked me to watch after his mother. We had lived like brothers; now he was asking me to adopt his mother. It was a backward kind of adoption, but at the moment it seemed the most natural thing in the world. He honored his mother by providing a surrogate son.

And I was all too happy to take on that role.

There weren't many of us who stood by the cross the day he died, but I never questioned where the others had gone. Love is like that. We simply give what we can to the one we love without comparing our relationship to another. I knew I had to be there. I stood at the foot of the cross alongside the others — mostly women. We stood there as an expression of our love.

It was a long time ago, and yet I remember standing at the foot of the cross like it happened yesterday. I remember the anguished cry and sense of abandonment that came from his lips. "My God, my God, why have you forsaken me," he cried as he quoted the psalmist (Mt. 27:46; Ps. 22:1). There have been times when I wished I could get the echo of his voice out of my mind, but more often I find great comfort in remembering that day — especially now as I find myself sitting in this isolated Roman penal colony, preparing for my own death, feeling my own sense of being abandoned by God.

I was imprisoned for proclaiming my love of Jesus and my belief in him. And now, as I await my destiny, I try to remember the grace with which he faced his own death. I want to die with as much grace and love as he did. I understand better now the sense of being forsaken by God, even though I know I am never alone. I also know the assurance of eternal life, a life that awaits me beyond the grave; it's an assurance that allows me to face the next day with certainty.

Maybe you've had similar experiences in your life, times when you wondered where God was or why God seemed to remain silent. Maybe you have experienced the pain of loss and grief or maybe it was an illness.

Maybe it was a time of decision-making where you felt alone. Maybe you are experiencing that today.

Believe me, I know that feeling. Here on the island of Patmos, we not only feel alone, we are alone. But there are two things I have learned in my time of isolation. First, being alone is not the same as being lonely. People can feel lonely when they are with others. To address the concerns of loneliness, I began to write — first my letters and then my gospel, and finally a record of the revelation I received here on Patmos.

But the other thing I learned is that God's silence is not the same as abandonment. We may feel alone, but God is very present. As the echo of his voice still rings in my ears, I know that Jesus experienced the sense of God's silence and the human doubts that accompany it. But he was not alone, neither am I, and neither are you.

When I consider the burdens and sorrows of my heart, I remember that Jesus carried a much heavier burden than I carry. And in that realization, I see how he has been walking ahead of me, leading me by his life and his example. If I learned nothing else from walking with him for three years in his earthly life, I am certain that he was always leading us, one step after the other.

I have followed him since I was a young man. Now I am old and I still find myself following in his footsteps. Christ is our brother, our older brother, who is revealing the promises of God in both his life and his death.

And I firmly believe what I wrote in the gospel, that people like you, people who live years and decades and centuries after me, people like you are more blessed than those of us who knew Jesus face to face (Jn. 20:29-31). You are truly the beloved children of God who also walk in his footsteps.

I was there when Jesus died, but my prayer continues to be, "Come quickly, Lord Jesus" (Rev. 22:20). Amen.

Longinus

Wow. Just hearing the story again takes me back to that place, even though I haven't worn the uniform of a Roman soldier for nearly twenty years. I had worked my way up to the point where I was supervising younger men and could see that there was a promotion awaiting me after what I thought would be a short stay in the territory of Judea — although it was even shorter than I had expected.

I had signed on with the Romans as a young man. It was my goal to serve long enough to earn my citizenship. You see, I was born in Cappadocia and I could see the distinct advantages of being a Roman in a world run by and controlled by the Romans. Our family would never have enough money to purchase my citizenship, so I enlisted in the military because of the promise of becoming a Roman citizen after I was released from service.

But on that day all I wanted to do was find a way out. I no longer wanted my name associated with what the Romans did, so I gave up the possibility of citizenship.

Don't get me wrong, I enjoyed most of the assignments I had been given. It was a privilege to travel from Rome to Spain and back to my country before being assigned to Judea. Prior to that assignment, I had served on guard details, protecting important people mostly, but occasionally working in prisons. I had enough free time to visit the local attractions and to learn about the various cultural differences within the Roman Empire. Everywhere I went, I marveled at the amazing road system that had been built primarily for the sake of the military. I loved seeing the beauty of the Mediterranean Sea from so many different locations, as well as the various forms of entertainment from the dramas to the horse races to the intellectual debates.

But this was the first assignment where I had been involved in putting men to death. It was an awful job. I hated this form of punishment, and I had a growing distaste for the way lives were simply cast aside by the whim of the governor.

And while I never liked being a part of the death squad, that day it was particularly difficult. Never had I seen such an anguished crowd, and never had I seen a man surrender himself to the process with such grace. He cried out to his God, but never did he seem angry with us. In fact, he prayed that God would forgive us for nailing him to the cross. (What kind of a response was that?) And then — and then the sky turned black as if all of heaven was joining in the grief of this one man's life. As the earth began to tremble, I became convinced this was no normal death. He was no normal man. He was the Son of God.

I had been a witness to the most profound event in history. I was so moved, in fact, that I surrendered my commission the next day and returned to my hometown. Citizenship was not worth compromising my own values. For years afterward I was haunted by the image of Jesus, dying in the darkness. Night after night, I would wake up to the sounds of that day. I could hear the sobbing of the women and the cowardly threats of his opponents. I still remember the moaning sounds of the dead as they walked among the living.

It still makes no sense to me. From where I stood, this was an innocent man being punished for speaking the truth to power. This was the Son of God. Who were we to pronounce judgment on him? And what would be the repercussions?

Every sleepless night filled me with more remorse for the part I played. I was there, although I wish I hadn't been. I wish that had been my day off. I wish I had been on leave. Of course, that might mean I would still be wearing a uniform. It might also mean I would already have my citizenship. But that isn't nearly as important to me now, especially since I know the price of citizenship is being paid by those who are not citizens.

I don't know if you've ever said something or done something you later regretted. Maybe it was an argument with your wife or your husband. Maybe it was the way you treated a co-worker. Maybe it was the way you ignored a plea for help. If you've ever been haunted by those kinds of events, you know what I was going through — except there seemed to be no end to my pain and sorrow.

I kept wishing I had taken a different stand. Maybe I could have helped him escape, for example. Maybe we could have found someone in the crowd who was truly guilty and condemned them in his place.

The truth is I didn't do what I knew to be the right thing. Instead I simply did what I was told to do. I participated in the sins of others and implicated myself as well. So I left in shame. I never wanted to face the people in that crowd again.

But I am here today because a man came to our town several years later and told me the incredible news that Jesus had been raised from the dead. He said that not only were my sins forgiven; there was also a place for me among his followers. He assured me that I would be given citizenship in the Kingdom of God — something that was of far more value than being a Roman citizen.

He knew I would be welcomed because he had spent a considerable amount of time persecuting these followers of Jesus himself! In fact, he suggested that God's Holy Spirit had been speaking through me when I first said, "Surely, this was the Son of God!" I had no idea how true my own words were.

Today people are risking their lives by claiming he is not only God's son, but Lord of their lives — both of which are direct violations of Roman law. They say it with confidence; and while I now say it with them, I find myself saying it with a twinge of guilt and a whole lot of humility.

Surely, this was the Son of God. And just as surely, I had participated in his crucifixion. I was there. I saw the blood and I heard the jeers of the crowds. I also heard the voice of Jesus crying out to God, "into your hands I commit my spirit" (Lk. 23:46).

I was there and I did nothing to stop it. In fact, I was the one responsible for making sure he died on that cross. It grieves me to remember his prayer for my forgiveness. It was a strange feeling to be forgiven by the man we were putting to death — especially when I realized he was the Son of God.

I quit my job because of what I had done — mostly because I wasn't ready to forgive myself. But I was forgiven by God; and not only that, maybe even more importantly, the church has welcomed me and forgiven me as well.

Just last week, in fact, I was working with a young man, John Mark. He was gathering stories so he could put them into a written account of the life of Jesus. He seemed particularly interested in my descriptions of the day Jesus died since so few people stayed to watch his final hours.

You see, Paul knew I was there, so he sent John Mark to me.

And I was there; although I wish I hadn't been. But I give thanks knowing it was for my sins that he died. Jesus asked God to forgive everyone who brought about his death — and I'm here today because I think that includes you, too. You see, anyone who has ever betrayed God, anyone who has ever said or done something they regret is no different than me; anyone who has remained silent in the face of injustice is no different than I am.

We all need to be forgiven.

And thanks be to God, we are.

SOLDIER

(Walking in with a robe in my arms.)

Martha! I'm home!

She must still be at the market. Oh yeah. I forgot this is Friday. And that means the markets will be closed tomorrow. Just one of the costs of living here rather than back home in Rome.

(Setting robe on the table. Touching it often during the discourse.)

She's going to be happy to see this, though! Usually when I'm on the execution squad, there isn't much left. I mean, I know sometimes people accuse us of being like vultures who devour the remnants of their lives, but most often no one else is there to claim their possessions.

And besides, vultures in nature provide an important function: they eat the rotting flesh, helping reduce the spread of disease.

It is ironic, though, because I joined the military because I thought of my role as a representative of the empire, an empire whose symbol is the eagle, not a vulture. We have a majestic and powerful history.

And part of our role is to bring our way of living to the backwaters of the empire.

And like many other parts of the empire, the people here need us. They need us to teach them how to change their way of living so they can become more like us. The whole reason we do these executions publicly is to teach them what is appropriate and acceptable behavior and what is just plain wrong. We do our best to deter others from repeating the crimes of those we execute — and to help them become better citizens in general.

In all honesty, sometimes I think we'd be better off getting rid of the whole lot of them. I'm not sure they'll ever learn how to live like civilized Roman citizens. They have some strange laws they insist on keeping, including a day when no one works once a week. Who ever heard of such a thing?

And then there is the sense of shame and guilt that comes with being hanged on a tree. They act as though the people are cursed for the way they die rather than the way they had been living! I'm not sure they'll ever figure out how to live right.

Our public executions are intended to help them learn how to live differently so they don't need to die.

It's funny, really. These Jews have some weird laws that make them think being in contact with a dead body contaminates them. They call themselves "unclean" and can't be with other people until they have gone through some ritual. So no one comes around to watch them die — for fear that they might get too close. Not even the people who cared about them witness the execution. So Martha takes these scraps of what is left from their lives and makes them into quilts and drapes and then sells them in their market places.

They have no idea where they came from or they'd probably never buy one!

Usually, it's just a few strips of cloth and an occasional piece of jewelry. But this one is different! Even the rest of the squad noted what an exquisite robe it is. So rather than dividing it equally between us, we rolled the dice — and I won!

But this particular prisoner was different, too. He actually had friends there. I can't remember that happening before.

But it was more than that.

Most days I work at the prison gates. I make sure they don't open — except to let prisoners in and those rare occasions when prisoners are taken out. Once a month I leave the gate and help with executions. Today was my day.

Most of the prisoners scream and yell. They spit in our faces and they fight with us all the way from the prison gates to the execution site, the place of the skull. It almost always takes three of us to get them there. And by the time we wrestle them down onto the cross, we've worked up such a sweat and are so weary of the fight that we find relief when the nails finally keep them still without us having to fight them.

Our only "reward" we can claim is the clothing they have — and sometimes there isn't enough to make it worth it.

But this prisoner was different — and not just because of this fine robe.

He looked in my eyes as if he were trying to see what I was thinking. He acted like he really cared about me — even though we'd never met. He freely and gently laid his hand out for me. And as I was getting ready to nail him to the cross, he said he forgave me.

I have to tell you, it was the first time I ever questioned what we were doing. The way he died made me wonder if the way he lived was better than the way I lived.

Most of the time, I am convinced we are doing an important service for Caesar and for the empire. We are ridding the neighborhoods of villains; they are thieves and murderers and everyone is better off without them.

But this man — and this robe — got me to questioning everything.

And then he said something familiar.

Once in a while, not very often, while guarding the gates, someone will come asking to release a prisoner. The official decree usually indicates that their time of imprisonment is over. They are not being kept for a capital crime and since their punishment is over, they are now free to go. (Personally, I think we should execute them all because I have no doubt they will be coming back.)

But the words used to indicate the completion of their sentence are the very words this man used on the cross: "It is finished."

Most of the time when those words are said, there is a sense of joy on the part of the prisoner who hears them. Families come and celebrate. But today, this man said it as if he were setting *me* free!

He forgave me and then he freed me.

It is finished.

But it's not! I need his friends and his family to forgive me, too.

And they probably should get his robe back, too. Martha will never know —

(Grabbing robe and rushing out the door.)

PETER

What can I say?
I should have been there. But I wasn't.
I should have said I was one of his followers.
Instead I denied it.
I should have said I knew him. But I was afraid.
Can you imagine that? I was the one who ventured out to walk on the water with Jesus (Mt. 14:21). I was the one who drew a sword when they came to arrest him (Jn. 18:10). But later that same night I denied I even knew him.

I had three chances to answer the question; and each time I made the wrong choice. When the cock crowed, it was like a mirror had been held up and I saw who I really was. That's when I left — in shame.

For the next day and a half, I wandered around in a gloomy daze. If I had said something different, I wondered, would I have died with him? On the other hand, if I had stood up for him, would he be free? If they ever put me on a cross, I hope they make it clear that I don't deserve to die with the dignity that he did — I hope they hang me up-side-down so everyone will know that he died so we could live, and not the other way around.

I spent the better part of three years with him; why couldn't I find a way to at least stand by him as his life was poured out on that cross?

When he needed me the most, I wasn't there. That happened when he was praying in the Garden of Gethsemane, too. He was praying with intensity like I've never seen before — and I kept dozing off (Lk. 22:45-46).

When I first met Jesus people called me Simon. I know you don't pay attention to it the way we did, but that name means "God has heard." God was listening to our pleas and our prayers. And when Jesus met me, he implied that my name's meaning had been fulfilled. God was listening and had sent us a savior. Because of that, he began to call me Peter, a name that means rock.

It's a name that suggested I was dependable so people could trust me. But on that day I felt more like quick sand than a rock. I was shying away when I should have been standing firm. All I could do was hope that God hadn't heard me. But even if God wasn't listening, Jesus had looked at me as if he knew what I had said — and what I didn't say (Lk. 22:61).

I have to confess to you that like Judas, I almost decided the world was better off without me. I had betrayed my own name; I had denied knowing the man who gave my life meaning. When it came time for courage, I ran away like a coward.

That's why I wasn't there the day he died.

It's also what I remembered the day Barnabas asked if he could bring Paul to meet us (Acts 9:27). Paul was a wretched man who had persecuted us because of our belief in Jesus. He stood by while Stephen was stoned to death (Acts 8:1). But we had heard there was a change in his heart.

Barnabas wanted to introduce him to us so we could see how he had changed. Barnabas believed Paul could be used by God — if we would find a way to welcome him into the fellowship of the church.

I kept thinking that if I could be welcomed back after what I had done, perhaps Paul could also be changed by the grace of God.

In fact, I often thought that if Judas had waited until Easter he, too, might have experienced that kind of change. So we met with Paul, and as the saying goes, the rest is history.

I don't know how much you remember about the teachings of Jesus. One time he referred to the scripture where it says that "the stone the builders rejected became the chief cornerstone" (Ps. 118:22). Jesus spoke about it in a way that suggested his own ministry had been rejected by the religious leaders, a ministry that was both accepted by and pleasing to God (Lk. 20:17).

I have often remembered that day and wondered if he wasn't really talking about me, Peter, the Rock, the one who rejected Jesus only to be used by God as the foundation of the church was being laid.

I guess it could have been Paul he was speaking about.

Maybe it was really a message for anyone who chooses to follow Christ. No matter what others may think, no matter what *we* may think, God can use us. We may be rejected by others, but God will make us a key part of the church. We may feel inadequate to the task, but God will work through us so that God's power is seen in us.

I'm not proud of the fact that I denied Jesus three times the night he was arrested. But one day after Easter, Jesus met us on the beach (Jn. 21:1-14). He took me aside to ask me if I loved him. I told him I did.

He asked me again if I loved him, and I assured him that I did. The third time he asked, I realized Jesus was giving me a chance to answer differently than I had before. This time I answered correctly.

After accepting my answer, Jesus told me that my task was to tend the sheep of his flock (Jn. 21:15-17). It didn't erase the memory of what I had done earlier, but it was clearly a time when I experienced forgiveness.

You see, I wasn't there at the foot of the cross. And every time I think about it, I remember my absence. I should have been there. In fact, I often think it should have been me on that cross.

But if it had been me, we wouldn't have Easter.

It's true that I deserved to die for the sin I had committed, but I wasn't there.

Several weeks after Easter, God's Holy Spirit filled me with power and I found my voice (Acts 2:14). It was as if I suddenly realized the truth of what happened at Easter — and I could not stop telling others about it. God came to set us free from sin.

I also know that if God can use me — the one who had a chance to say "yes" but instead said "no" — then God can use you. All you have to do is open your heart and let his love fill you and flow through you.

He died on the cross so we could live. It is now up to those of us who follow him to sustain and nurture others on their journey.

I wasn't there that day, but I know that on the cross Jesus bore my sin so that I might live. And he did the same for you.

Thanks be to God.

Amen.

Voices in Advent & Christmas

I don't know how it is for other pastors and preachers, but the season of Advent and Christmas have always been difficult for me. The texts are familiar, there are high expectations of dynamic sermons, and it is hard to find ways to present the story in new ways.

A few times I tried to enter the story from one of the characters in the story. Included here are three examples where I donned the role of one of those characters and spoke in the first person. The congregational settings varied, but each of the sermons was well-received.

JOSEPH

You know, and I know, that if I had lived in your world things would have been different. But we didn't know about DNA. We had no way to do a paternity test. For millennia, in fact, we were sure who a child's mother was. But there was no way to prove who the father was.

Probably one of the first times that question was raised was when Tamar became pregnant. I know, for many of you, she is just a name listed in my genealogy (Mt. 1:3). I'll let you read the story to learn how it came to be there (Gen. 38). What's important to hear today is that Judah claimed paternity of her twin sons, Perez and Zerah.

Without that claim, they would have been ostracized and excluded — and who knows what would have become of them? It's almost certain that Tamar, their mother, would have lived in poverty all of her days.

Instead, she became one of King David's ancestors. Without her, he would not have been born. Without Judah's intervention, he could not have become King. And me? I would just be another one of the many people in the occupied territory of Judea instead of being a descendent of the King, a potential heir to the throne of David.

Since I was a youth, I had been told that being a son of David meant I should do whatever I could to avoid controversy, to live an upright life, to learn the law and to abide by the law. I was taught to attend worship and to give generously, to live as if I was worthy of inheriting the throne.

So, when Mary came to me with her news, I found myself caught. Her story could become a mark on my character. At the same time, I knew there had to be a way I could help her, even though I knew the child wasn't mine.

I have to tell you, though, I didn't sleep much that night.

During the night, I remembered the story of Tamar and how Judah helped her (Gen. 38:25-26). I remembered the laws regarding faithfulness to marriage (including Ex. 20:14; 22:16). I remembered the laws that allowed for divorce and the reasons we were allowed to do so, including during the engagement period (Dt. 22:23-24; 24:1).

I also remembered the story of Joseph, for whom I had been named. He found himself in several different situations where God showed him the way out.

You've probably heard some of those stories, too, haven't you?

- He was thrown into a pit and didn't lose hope (Gen. 37:24).
- He was sold into slavery and continued to live an upright life (Gen. 39:1).
- He was falsely accused and yet he managed to hold his head high (Gen. 39:14).
- Eventually he became the savior of our people because he earned the respect of

Pharaoh and successfully managed his storehouses so we survived a drought (Gen. 45:7).

It happened often enough that I began to wonder if God would show me a way out of my dilemma.

Then, just like the Joseph who was my ancestral uncle, I found myself dreaming (Gen. 37:5; Mt. 1:20). It was both frightening and comforting. It was really strange, too. The angel told me not to be afraid. And then assured me that I was chosen as the one to claim the baby as my child so that he would be considered a son of David, just as I had been.

I was also told to name him Jesus, a name that means savior (Mt. 1:21).

In all honesty, I didn't know for sure that it would work.

But I accepted my role as a foster parent. Actually, in our culture when the father gives a name for the child he is claiming paternity. In some ways, it felt as though I was adopting this child. At the same time, I knew it was more than that. It was almost like he was adopting me!

I mean, I grew up learning the importance of the scriptures and praying and attending worship. And I grew up learning the trade of my father. So, it wasn't hard to practice what I had experienced. I taught Jesus the importance of the scriptures and how to pray and made sure he was attending worship. I taught him the trade I had learned from my father.

But sometimes it felt like I was the one who was learning.

We made regular pilgrimages to Jerusalem, something many of my neighbors were too busy to accomplish more than once or twice in a lifetime. We made the trip as often as we could, leaving behind our work to worship. Several of those trips were memorable.

I remember on one of our first trips, soon after Jesus was born, people noticed him and prayed for him and blessed him (Lk. 2:22). In a strange way, it confirmed that the dreams were real.

On another trip, I almost lost it and yelled at Jesus for making us worry — because he stayed behind when we left (Lk. 2:43). I know he knew the importance of obeying his parents; and yet he was fascinated by the conversations of the rabbis. And when we found him I realized he had much to teach me.

I was teaching him the rules God had given us for living. But he was showing me how to live within those rules. I was teaching him how to love and at the same time he was showing me that love had different limits than I once thought. I was teaching him how to work with wood and he was teaching me that the things we were making were for families and our focus should be on the recipient of the product, not the product itself.

I remember teaching him the stories of Elijah. We would talk about the miracles he performed and how he stood up to the false prophets. But Jesus helped me see that Elijah helped the Gentiles in the story and suggested that God loved all the people, not just our people (Lk. 4:25-27).

I remember telling him the story of the Passover. And when I told him about Moses leading the people through the Red Sea, Jesus asked, "Do you think God cried because of the Egyptians who died that day?"

I remember telling him about the Messiah that was to come, the one who would eventually claim the throne of our father David. In the synagogue, as the stories were read, we would pray for the deliverance from the Roman oppressors. (Of course, I wondered if Jesus was indeed that person.)

But Jesus asked us about the servant Isaiah mentions and how the Messiah suffered, how he was beaten and yet never spoke a word (Is. 53:3-5). He also reminded us that Isaiah called Cyrus the Messiah, a man who was a Gentile (Is. 45:1).

And you've probably heard how he re-told Ezekiel's story of the good shepherd (Ezek. 34; Jn. 10).

He was constantly and consistently helping us see that our faith was more than genetics, more than something into which we were born. It is a lifestyle, a way of living, a way of relating to others so that God's story can be seen and heard in our stories.

I did not live to see his life unfold, but I know the story. I also know that I taught him and in teaching him, I found him teaching me. And what I learned was that knowing the right answers is not as important as a lifestyle based on those answers.

And today, I want you to know that truth still applies.

The story of my son will not change anyone's life unless and until you learn to live in such a way that you don't need to speak. Others will see your compassion. Others will know you have reached out to them. People will see when you cross the boundaries of the familiar and include those who are often left out.

Never confuse silence with inaction, though. There are times when it is important to do something, whether it's offering food to the hungry or standing to protest unjust laws. (Which I hear many of you already do.)

Faith is not about having the right answers; it's not about being heavenly minded, either. It's about a lifestyle that reflects grace; it's about living a down to earth lifestyle that reveals the power of God's love.

And as we say in my tradition:

So be it.

Luke 2:1-20

Amos

I thought Sarah would understand. I knew many wouldn't, but I surely thought my wife would. She just said, "You really are getting to be a silly old man, Amos. Maybe you're too old to be out with the sheep."

I wonder if some of you will believe me? I suppose some will and some won't. Anyway, I'll tell you what happened. It was the most wonderful moment of my life! And to think that I, old Amos, was one of those to have such a night! It was the night of all nights!

I'll tell you what happened. My two old friends, Jonathan and Isaac, and Isaac's young grandson, Ezra, and I were out in the fields with the sheep. It was cold and we were all huddled into our cloaks talking quietly, when young Ezra jumped up shouting, "Look, look! Angels!"

And there were angels! Lots of them in the sky! Shining and bright! And there was music like I never heard! Ezra was frightened and ran to his grandfather, throwing his arms around his waist, saying, "Grandfather, Grandfather, what's happening?"

Then the angel said to us — his exact words are etched in my mind — "Do not be afraid; for see — I am bringing you good news of great joy for all the people: to you is born this day in the city of David a Savior, who is the Messiah, the Lord. This will be a sign for you: you will find a child wrapped in bands of cloth and lying in a manger."

At first we were all terrified, and then a deep peace came over me — and *I knew*! I knew that the day I had prayed for every day of my life had come. Hadn't the prophet Micah said that the Messiah would come out of Bethlehem? I said to my startled companions, "Let's go to Bethlehem and see this thing that has taken place, which the Lord has made known to us."

As we trudged to the village, I kept thinking. A baby?! I thought he'd be a man! In a manger?! Seems a strange place for a king! But I remembered what I had heard last Sabbath in the synagogue from the scroll of Isaiah, "For my thoughts are not your thoughts, nor are your ways my ways, says the Lord." (Is 55:8)

You know, I am an old man, and through all these years I've found out that surely God's ways are not mine — but they are right and so much better.

As we stood in that stable and looked at the newborn baby the angels told us about, we three old shepherds knew that God had answered our prayers — just in a different way than we had expected.

The next day, I hurried to the rabbi to tell him about the wondrous event.

I couldn't believe it when he laughed at me, and told me I was having hallucinations. "Too much old wine for an old man," he said. "If God was going to send angels to announce the Messiah, he would have sent them to me, the rabbi, not to you shepherds in the field. The Messiah will not come as a baby and certainly not in a stable. Go home Amos and rest."

But I couldn't rest at home, either. Then there was Sarah, my wife; and she couldn't believe it either.

And young Ezra! He was shaken by the rabbi's disbelief. He asked his grandfather, "Grandfather, we did see angels, didn't we?" His grandfather told him,

"Yes, my grandson, we did see them." Then he asked me, "Amos, is it really true? Is this really the Messiah come as a baby? Is it true?"

And I told him — and myself — "*Yes, it is really true!*"

And I tell you. It is true. It's surely true.

Yes, it is true. It's surely true.

Thanks be to God. It's true.

BALTHAZAR

My name is Balthazar, and I want to tell you about a journey I made a long, long time ago; a trip that changed my life.

The sky was dark the night we started. There was no moon, and the clouds of the winter sky obscured even the stars. I remember the darkness so well because we laughed about the irony of it. We were going west because we'd seen this star; and our first night out, there were no stars at all . . . not one could pierce through the dark clouds.

Melchior had seen the star first. It was a new star, rising in the western sky . . . a relatively bright star.

We were astrologers — not as you know them, but the ancient equivalent of your scientists. Many people called us *magi*.

Your word 'magic' comes from 'magi'. But I want you to know that we were not tricksters. We were not pretenders. We were honest and deliberate. We read the stars for signs and interpreted them.

In some ways, I suppose, you could also call us philosophers.

When this new star appeared in the western sky; our books told us that it was the star of a king, a Hebrew king.

Casper suggested that we visit this king. At first we laughed at him, but in time, we caught his vision. Perhaps it was the long and dark winter days that made travel sound appealing. The prospect of seeing new places; of learning new truths . . . sent us packing.

We rented some camels, hired some experienced camel drivers, and packed special gifts for the king. And we set off at night, in the direction of the star we could no longer see.

It was to be quite an adventure, a journey we'd never forget. We should have been excited about the trip. But the trip itself was a disaster!

Have you ever ridden a camel? It isn't like riding a horse, you know. On a horse, you ride proud and comfortable. You can become a part of the animal and be very graceful. Not so on a camel. You hang on for dear life, you go up and down, up and down, up and down. At times, the camels become stubborn and you walk. Nothing graceful about that.

And then there's the smell! I can still remember the stink of it all.

And that wasn't the worst of it. Dust! Our journey caused us to face into the wind of the desert dust. Our mouths were constantly dry, our eyes were irritated.

It was a miserable trip. Even if we had left the camel drivers out!

These must have been the most disgusting men I had ever met! They cursed and grumbled, they drank and gambled; why, they made us stay in the most hostile towns and villages so they could chase women longer!

We didn't dare spend much time with the camel drivers — especially when they started to laugh about our trip. We became the brunt of their jokes and were constantly subjected to their derision and scorn.

It was awful!

The only redeeming factor among the camel drivers was a blanket one of them had woven from camel hair. It was simply beautiful! He carried it with him on every caravan he had ever been a part of. He had taken time to weave it himself, with elaborate patterns and striking colors. It was large enough to use as a bedroll all by itself, with enough to protect you from the sand below and the wind above.

And I wanted it. I offered to buy it, but he refused. My offering price kept getting higher and higher.

But he would not part with it. "It is a part of who I am," he said. "You can have it when I die."

(I must confess, I hoped he would die... it would give us some peace with one less camel driver and I would receive the added benefit of this beautiful blanket.)

But the worst part of the trip wasn't the camels; it wasn't the desert dust; it wasn't even the camel drivers.

The hardest part was the doubt.

We stopped telling innkeepers why we were travelling or where we were going because they always laughed. They called us the three stooges.

As the dark days stretched on, one into another, we began to wonder what supposedly wise men were doing following a star. At least I wondered. We never talked about it. It got to where we didn't talk much at all. We watched for the star at dusk, this star of wonder, and we wandered on.

And we wondered.

What if there was no king? What would people say about us? Our whole livelihood was hanging in the balance. If there was no king, no one would ever come to us again. We would be out of work!

When we finally arrived in the land of the Jews, we went to Jerusalem because it was their temple city. I know now how silly it sounds, but we had no idea that Herod and the Jews were mortal enemies living side-by-side. We went to the royal authority — King Herod, the Roman governor and asked about this new born king.

I knew it was a mistake as soon as we met Herod. He struck me as a weasel. I simply didn't like him.

We asked our simple, innocent question . . . and then the fireworks started! I could tell by the red color in his neck and the anger in his eyes and his hurried manner as he left us that we had made a grave mistake. It was either the wrong question, or the wrong place, or the wrong time. But it was wrong. Dead wrong. Maybe our journey had been a mistake after all.

When he came back, Herod was all smiles and smoothness. He had asked his advisors about the new born king, and they had informed him that the child was to be born in a little town called Bethlehem.

"Come back after you've found him," he said sweetly. "I'll have my cooks prepare a meal for you when you return; and dry lodging for a night or two. You can tell me all about the child, where he is staying so that I, too, may go and pay him tribute."

I still didn't like him. But we thanked him kindly and went on our way.

We were greatly disappointed when we arrived in Bethlehem. It was such a poor town, and so small. No place for a king!

But it seemed the star was going there, too, so we went.

It was not at all what we expected. When we found the house, it looked too ordinary. We nearly went on, but Melchior said we'd come a long way so we might as well see what there was to see.

What we saw was a baby and his mother and father looking for all the world like an ordinary Hebrew family; except maybe poorer. Mary was baking barley cakes; Joseph was gathering wood. The baby was asleep.

Our gifts seemed so inappropriate. This family needed food and clothing, not frankincense and myrrh! But Mary graciously accepted them.

We told her about the star; and that we believed it was the star of a king, and that somehow the star had led us to her and to her son.

Mary didn't seem surprised. It was the first time we had told our story without hearing laughter or seeing disbelief in the eyes of the hearer.

We stayed a while, but the baby soon woke and we knew it was time to leave.

I wanted to go back to Herod. I thought we could play a trick on him. But Melchior had a bad dream and so we thought it was much safer for us and for the child to go home the other way.

I don't remember much about the trip home. It seemed to pass quicker. It was less miserable. The towns seemed friendlier. The dust almost seemed sweet to taste.

Even the camel-drivers were more pleasant to be with.

But I was curious when I realized that the blanket was missing, so I asked the camel-driver about it. He explained how when he saw the child and remembered how we had said he was a king, he wanted to offer something to him. So he gave the child what he had, his most prized possession. He said he felt better having given it to the baby.

Somehow, our story had made a difference in his life. It's funny, I never thought much about it until then.

But I know it changed my life, too. Casper began calling the trip our "Wild Goose Chase." It seemed to him that we had traveled a mighty long way to see a nursing baby.

I tried to explain it to him, but it's like a good joke — if you have to explain it, it isn't funny.

"Somehow", I tried to explain, "I saw the very face of God in that child's face."

The irony of our gifts was also clear to me: this was a gift from God, as significant as the gift of life itself. Nothing could compare — not even gold seemed appropriate. The camel driver's blanket was much more appropriate — not because the family was poor, but because it was a part of the giver.

You see, I now know that the only appropriate gift for this child is to give him your heart, as I did — not in Bethlehem, but somewhere on our return journey.

I no longer find comfort in studying the stars. I want to spend my time telling the world that God has come into the world. I want everyone to be able to see that child's face, to experience that star that we followed so diligently.

And my prayer for you today, my friends, is that you will see the star yourself, that it will lead you to the face of the child, and that you will experience the gift that God has given to you.

It's a gift beyond price, and it's been given to you.

Thanks be to God.

Amen.

OTHER VOICES

Throughout the scripture, there are characters whose voices kept speaking to me. I put some of their stories into my voice and spoke from the pulpit as if I were the character being described.

Often, there is little support for the story. Sometimes there is barely a mention of the character, let alone the name! These sermons were preached in a variety of settings over the course of two decades. Almost always people found themselves connecting with the characters.

The last sermon is perhaps my favorite in this genre, even though it is one of the oldest. It is the only one where the voice comes from an object rather than a person. That one is based on a purely fictional musing as I tried to envision the scene I was reading.

LOT

Hi. My name is Lot, and I'd like to tell you a story about my aunt and uncle, Sarai and Abram. I was basically raised by Sarai and Abram. They had no children, and I was the only child of Abram's brother, Haran. My father died when I was young.

It was about the time that my father died that my grandfather, Terah moved from Ur where the rest of our family had lived and died (Gen. 11:31). (Ur is in what is now called Iraq). Grandpa Terah had intended to move as far as Canaan, but when we arrived in a place called Haran, he decided to settle there. (I always suspected it was because the place reminded him of my father and the grief kept him from going any further.)

In those days, it was important to have children, since they were to look after you in your old age. That meant that Abram had to care for Terah. Since I had no father, I assumed the role of caring for Abram and Sarai who had no children.

Life was tough in those days. Food was scarce at times and caravanners would come and steal what little we had if we were not careful. But we managed.

I remember when Grandpa Terah died. It was a lonely time for all of us. Our family was fast dwindling and soon there would only be me. Abram was getting old and it meant that I did more of the work. At least I tried to do more of the work.

Abram insisted on doing his share — even though he was well past 70 years old!

Not long after Terah's funeral, Abram announced that we would move. We would leave Haran, but not to return to Ur as I would have liked, but to continue the journey to Canaan that Terah had begun. I had never been to Canaan, but it sounded like a beautiful place from what we had heard people say.

It also sounded like a **long** way to go. Especially at their age!

Quite frankly, I thought it was a stupid idea. They were both too old to be moving. It made me wonder if he was losing his mind! Especially when he began to attribute his decision to some God that I had never heard of! But I had learned at a young age to respect my elders. So we headed off for some strange land with nothing.

And I mean *nothing*!

- We had no family.
- We had no servants.
- We had no cattle or sheep.
- We had no camels.

We just had ourselves and this so-called promise that Abram kept referring to:

> "Go . . to the land that I will show you. I will make of you a great nation, and I will bless you, and make your name great, so that you will be a blessing. I will bless those who bless you, and the one who curses you I will curse; and in you all the families of the earth shall be blessed" — Gen. 12:1-3

How could this be?

Abram had no children. How could he ever become "a great nation"? Nations are made up of many tribes, and tribes are made up of many clans, and clans are made up of many families, and families are made up of many children. Abram only had a wife and a nephew. How did he ever expect us to become a nation?!!

Not that I doubted that Abram could become a great person that people all over would respect and admire. I figured his name would become great. He had a warm heart and a kind smile that made everyone feel important. I could easily see how this man could become well known by the travelers and caravanners we met. I could see how he could even become a legend with his generosity and hospitality. I know he bailed me out of trouble when I needed it!

I remember the time that I was captured and taken into slavery. Abram gathered some people up and rescued me (Gen. 14:13-16)! Of course I was family, so that may not help you understand the extent of his generosity and self-giving.

There was the other story I remember him telling me about, though. Three strangers appeared at his tent one day. Abram insisted that they stay for a small meal. Then he had Sarai provide a feast for them (Gen. 18:1-8). He didn't want them to leave and feel as though he had not offered them as much as they needed or wanted!

And, true to his nature, Abram spoke about the incident later as if he had met God that day!

In fact, he sounded ridiculous when he announced that the visitors had promised that he and Sarai would have a child within the year (Gen. 18:9-15)! Not only did Sarai laugh, but the story brought the rest of us to tears! How could someone who was nearly a hundred years old have a child?

My uncle believed the unbelievable. He was too naïve to ever ask a question and challenge the most obvious impossibilities.

But in the end, it was I who had erred.

Abram's God did not fail him.

Even when we arrived in Canaan and were forced to go south because of famine, it seemed as though his God had gone before him, protecting him and directing his steps (Gen. 20:1-17). And when I was living in Sodom, it was Abram who prayed that my life would be spared! He not only listened to his God, but his God listened to him (Gen. 18:22-33)!

And what is amazing to me, as I tell people about my uncle, is that Abram insisted that he didn't do anything that made God choose him. He simply opened his ears to God and obeyed the voice he heard. In Abram's own eyes and as he told the story to me, the promises came before any commands or directives. God simply promised to be his God, to bless him, and to bring prosperity to him and the whole world through him.

I know that my own life was blessed by Abram and Sarai.

And I suspect that yours has too — even if you do not realize it fully.

More importantly, I learned from Abram about this God of grace who offers to bless us and then invites us to serve as witnesses of this love and grace. It all begins here. It all begins now. God offers us the gift of eternal life and asks us to share the wonder and glory of this gift with others.

I don't know how you will respond to so rich a gift.

For me, well, I remember how Abram responded: "So Abram went, as the LORD had told him (Gen. 12:4a)."

Genesis 22:1-5*a*

HEZRON

You don't know me.

You won't find my name in your Bible either.

My name is Hezron. My father was Abraham's trusted servant, Eliezer of Damascus (Gen. 15:2).

My father met him when Abraham was traveling from his home in Ur. He was known as Abram then, but everyone who met him knew he was special (Gen. 17:5). He had those piercing eyes that made you tremble whenever he looked at you. But he was so compassionate, so caring, that anyone and everyone who knew him almost stumbled over each other trying to help him.

My father had been orphaned and found work wherever he could. That's how he happened to be at the main meeting place in Damascus that night when Abraham and his company arrived. Hoping he might be paid for his efforts, my father offered to care for their animals while they found a place to rest.

No one was interested in hosting him, though. Instead Abraham was cast out onto the street with his animals. I think he scared people. He kept talking about a God who sent him from his home to a land he had never seen. People don't like it when people talk crazy like that.

But Abraham never seemed crazy to me. And because my father had been so kind, Abraham invited him to join them when they left Damascus, and he jumped at the chance. That's how we ended up being a part of his family. In hindsight, I can see now that God was providing for us before we even knew who God was.

Abraham was always reaching out and welcoming strangers, providing meals, shelter and a shady place to rest (see Gen. 18:1-8, for example). You probably already heard the story about the Egyptian woman he welcomed into our community. Hagar became the servant for his wife Sarah (Gen. 16:1).

As a consequence, I grew up in a multi-ethnic community, a place where it seemed that anyone who was not welcome elsewhere was always welcome. And in that community I learned from a young age that God was always able to provide for us — although it didn't always come the way we expected.

My father tells about entering Canaan where they began to raise sheep. It was a land where no one else had been able to survive for very long, but God provided and we prospered.

One time, when there was a drought, Abraham was certain God would provide for them. He prayed for rain. He watched the horizon day after day, week after week, month after month. Then one day, a relative of Hagar came and told him about the lush land in Egypt (Gen. 12:10). Abraham realized God was providing a safe place for us — just not the way he thought God would do it.

Another time was when Abraham's nephew was captured in war. He hadn't chosen a good place to live, and when two kings began to wage war, Abraham prayed for Lot's safety. When the war ended, Lot was gone — along with everyone and everything in his town. But Abraham was able to gather some people together and God was able to give that rag tag little army the strength to overcome the enemy and rescue him (Gen. 14:14-16).

Now, those were stories my father told. I was too little to remember them. But in time I became convinced God would provide, too.

For a long time, my father thought he and I would inherit the accumulating wealth of Abraham. After all, Sarah had no children and we were the most trusted of the families who worked for Abraham. But then God provided a son — well, sort of.

Ishmael was not Sarah's son, but he was Abraham's (Gen. 16:3-4). I felt sorry for him, though. He and I were almost the same age, but it was clear from the time we were little that Sarah didn't much care for him. Had it not been for Abraham, I'm not sure he would have lived with us as long as he did (compare Gen. 16:6 with 17:18 or read Gen. 21:9-11).

When Isaac was born, things changed. Sarah began to laugh and Abraham lost the furrow in his brow (Gen. 21:6). Abraham must have been 100 years old, but he played with his son as if he were a young man (Gen. 21:5).

Of course, Ishmael was eventually sent away (Gen. 21:14). And it just occurred to me that God provided for Ishmael and Hagar, too (Gen. 21:19).

One day, Abraham decided to go on a journey (Gen. 22:2-5). With him, he took my father and me, along with Isaac. We took turns leading the donkey as we walked. It was there that I learned the details of how my father had met Abraham. It was there that I learned how often God had provided for Abraham and how many times Abraham had actually welcomed people into his home — almost as if he knew God was using him to meet their needs.

When we could see a mountain not too far away, Abraham asked us to stop and unload the donkey. Then he loaded the wood onto his son's back and asked us to remain with the donkey. Isaac was all too happy to carry the load, but Abraham seemed to walk away with a stoop in his back as if he were carrying the heavier burden.

My father and I waited for several days. And each day I began to worry more.

When we began this journey, I thought we were going on a holy pilgrimage. We had everything we needed to make a sacrifice — everything except a lamb, that is. But I figured God would provide one (Gen. 22:8).

Just as Abraham and Isaac walked out of my vision, it occurred to me that maybe, just maybe, Isaac was going to be the sacrifice. Maybe Abraham was bent over because of what he planned to do.

I mean, it wasn't unheard of. We knew of neighboring clans and tribes that made periodic rituals out of taking their children and giving them to their gods.

But Abraham was always so kind; I couldn't imagine him doing such a thing. Abraham welcomed strangers and outcasts because he knew we were all precious in God's sight. It would have been out of character for him to do such a thing.

But with each passing day, I worried more.

All day long I strained my eyes at the horizon hoping I would see two people returning from the mountain, not one.

He wasn't my son. And if he died, I might inherit what would be his; but still I was more afraid for him than I had ever been afraid before. The sound of my heart beating often kept me from hearing any other sound as we waited and wondered.

I don't know what my father thought. He never spoke. I would ask my questions aloud, but he acted as though I had said nothing. He simply waited with patience. I suppose it's because he knew God had provided in the past and was convinced God would do so again.

I startled him when I jumped and whooped! I saw them coming! Father and son, walking hand in hand, standing upright and tall. They were smiling together as they walked.

God had provided for them after all — in a way I hadn't expected.

Isaac told me some of the details on the way home. But for the first time I understood why the people in Damascus were afraid of Abraham. He was so certain about the things God told him to do that no matter what he was asked, Abraham simply responded in obedience. His faith seemed to know no bounds.

And God provided again and again.

But I have to confess that I don't always wait as patiently as my father did or as confidently as Abraham did. But in my better days, I look for ways God is providing for me — with an eye toward those places where God may be providing in ways I don't expect.

I guess God is still doing that. I heard that this week God helped make it possible for a meeting to end early. It was unexpected, but God was at work.

And while I don't always wait as patiently as I could, I usually do find time to give thanks to God when my needs are met.

But I'll bet you do that, too.

Thanks for listening to my story.

And remember, God will provide. But it may not be the way you expect.

Shalom.

MICA

I am convinced that the sin of David is the sin of the whole people of Israel. In fact, I am convinced that the sin of anyone is the sin of everyone. I also admit I am somewhat bitter with my King David over what has happened, but I am becoming aware of the fact that he is not the only sinner in the kingdom. Whenever any of us is guilty of sin, we are all guilty of sin.

I didn't always think that. It has been developing in my mind ever since that fateful event. An event which not only changed my life, but affected everyone in the Kingdom of Israel.

Sometimes I wish I could go back to the days before we moved to Jerusalem. Those were simpler times, if not as comfortable. My grandfather, Jonathon, had found a nice area for us to live and had taken every precaution to protect us from the violence and the upheaval that was so much a part of life in those days. King Saul was trying to protect his right to reign as King so that Jonathon would inherit the throne after his death. Of course, that was not to be.

Then came the turmoil over who would become King after both Saul and Jonathon died. It was clear in our minds that we were not serious contenders, but we never knew for sure. My father may have been crippled in the feet, but someone may have seen him as a threat and sought us out.

That is why we were extremely grateful for the assistance of Ziba, the servant that Saul and Jonathon had hired to care for us. Ziba knew that our enemies may seek us out and so he took every precaution to protect us.

We all breathed a heavy sigh of relief when the leaders of Israel sought out David and asked him to be King of all of Israel and Judah. No more killing. No more death. No more fear of someone coming to remove us from the Kingdom.

"Mica," my father had said to me, "we are safe now. We can begin to find enjoyment in life."

Imagine our surprise, our terror, when Ziba came and told us that David had been asking for us.

Ziba tried to comfort us by telling us the reason David had asked about us, but we were still a little fearful. We had lived in fear too long, I suppose, to believe that he was actually concerned for our well-being.

"You didn't tell him where we were, did you?" my father asked.

"Of course not. You know me well enough to know that I would not do that without your permission. I only told him that I would look and see if there was any trace of you to be found. I did not guarantee him anything."

Ziba tried to explain that David was concerned and wanted to honor his friend, my grandfather Jonathon, by caring for any of his descendants that may be alive. Ziba was certain that his motivations were pure.

And so we went.

Perhaps it was because of what Ziba told us, but my first impressions of King David were of an unassuming man with a large heart. He welcomed us into his presence with an embrace. He asked us to sit at his table. He actually treated us as royalty! We had not been treated that way in years.

Certainly, he was motivated by love. He was only seeking to serve God by caring for us.

Eventually, that care took the form of finding meaningful work for me — as a messenger of the King. It was not only meaningful, but exciting! I loved it!

O, but his palace was what struck me most when we arrived in Jerusalem. I will never forget the feeling of awe and wonder that overwhelmed me as I walked through those doors for the first time! I had never seen such wondrous things! High wooden doors. Polished floors. Marble furniture. Beautiful paintings on the walls. We had none of those things. We had mud walls, dirt floors, and what little furniture we had was roughly hewn out of rock or wood. We had a little pottery, but nothing to compare with the marvelous pieces in the King's palace.

I was only too glad to be with David. I had heard about his abilities to fight battles before. It was what made us so fearful at first. But we had also heard about his deep passion for life — even the life of his enemies. It was told that on more than one occasion he had killed the messenger who brought the news of the death of one of our family — people who were his supposed enemies! There was no one I would rather be with than David in those days!

I was especially excited when he allowed me to accompany him during the battles against the Syrians. To actually see him making decisions about who should go where, when to move forward, when to move back, and when to wait patiently for the enemy was probably the best education in military tactics anyone will ever receive.

It all seemed to fit in with what I had done when I was younger. While I knew that I would never become King, I made it a hobby of mine to know what the role of the King was, and David seemed to fit it better than I could imagine anyone fitting it. Certainly, he had his faults, but not anymore than anyone else would have had.

In Deuteronomy, Moses had warned us about desiring a king. But still we desired one. He had warned us that a king over us should be one of us, not a foreigner, and that he should not create a standing army with large numbers of horses and chariots, that he should not have too many wives for himself, that he should not create a large personal treasury. What Moses expected of the King was one who would keep a copy of the law close at hand to study and meditate upon day and night.

But when the cry went out for a king, it was not for any of that. It was so that we would be like all of the others nations! We wanted someone to fight battles and govern us. Even when David was finally acclaimed as King, it was because of his military leadership not because of his faithfulness to the law of Moses!

Not that he wasn't faithful to the law. David had a reputation as being very faithful to God. He wrote wonderful music and prayers for use in public worship. He even brought the Ark of the Covenant closer to the King's residence so that he could worship more often!

I don't mean to suggest that he was perfect, but everyone seemed to accept his faults as part of his job, part of his role. After all, we reasoned, he was King.

His standing army was not seen as a violation of Moses' law, but a necessity in a world where there are so many adversaries on so many sides. He needed them to have the clout in making treaties and arrangements with other kings and governors. And his wives? Well, each had their place in his life. He never let them run his life as Moses feared. Besides, some of them were simply wives of convenience, chosen for political purposes. No one would expect him to say no to those arrangements. They made the Kingdom more secure.

And as for his personal treasury, he had a standing policy that whenever an enemy was vanquished, each warrior received a fair share of the booty. His treasury was no larger than anyone else's. His house may have looked expensive, but it wasn't built by himself, but was a gift from the King of Tyre.

David may not have been the perfect example of what Moses said we should have for a king, but he did do everything we expected of him, and his sins were not so grievous that we could not overlook them.

At least not until the spring of the year when I began to see how we had implicated ourselves in his policies and attitudes.

David had sent the troops out under Joab's leadership and had remained behind. In fact most of the men over the age of twenty had gone to fight the battle. The only men in Jerusalem were newlyweds (who were exempt from military service), retirees, messengers for the King, such as myself, and King David.

I was a little naïve, perhaps, but I wasn't really sure what David was wanting when he asked who it was that lived in the house three blocks down and two houses over from the palace. I thought he was looking for another cook for the palace — God knows we needed one. But when I found out who she was, I had a gut feeling about what he really needed. This was the home of Bathsheba. Simply the most beautiful woman in all of Jerusalem.

Every man had given her lustful looks at one time or another — but only from a distance. No one dared rile her husband.

I really didn't want to believe my instincts. I began to make all sorts of excuses for David. He had a message for her father. Or her husband. He had a message from them for her. (No, that would have been the duty of one of us, the messengers to relay.)

If he was really thinking what I thought he was thinking, he needed to be warned. But how could I do that? I am only a messenger. I decided to tell him who she was — and to remind him that her father was one of his faithful warriors, Eliam — and then to remind him that her husband is one of the thirty noted warriors in all of Israel, Uriah. Perhaps he will take the subtle warnings and not act on his passions.

Imagine my surprise, my horror, when he asked me to bring her up to the palace. No, No, No, I thought. The King is not supposed to act this way! But what can I do? I paced back and forth outside her house for some time before I decided that I had no choice but to follow the King's commands. I could only hope that my intuition was wrong and that there was another explanation.

The next thing I knew, I was bringing a message to him. I was saddened, to say the least.

But I was terrified when I noticed Uriah was back in town. Had he heard what happened? Was he there to kill the King? Does David know that he is in town?

O, he would die if he knew what had been happening behind his back! But he didn't seem to know or care. He left a few days later. He never even went to his own house! (I had made sure David knew that he was safe by reporting that Uriah had not left the palace gate.)

But the worst was yet to come. Uriah died, and even before the mourning period was over, David had married Uriah's wife. No one knows what happened to Uriah, and only I know what happened to force the early marriage, but I am bitter towards David now. I have no more respect for the man. I only do what I am told to do and no more. I now wish I was back with Ziba, back in our own home.

But that would not help either. We have all sinned. We are all in this together. We asked David to be a king, but did not ask him to comply with the law. We gave him permission to break the law whenever it was convenient for him to do so. We are the ones who are at fault.

And it is not just David, either. Whenever any of us sins against God or against another person, we are all guilty. We all sin when we allow sin to exist around us. Whenever we condone an act of violence against another person, we commit the violent act ourselves. Whenever we tell a white lie, we let down the rest of the human race.

Our God demands more of us. Our God has set us aside as a special people, as a light to the world. Whenever we allow sin to exist in our midst, we dim the light. Dim it too much, and there is no light left.

And don't allow yourself to think I am only talking about the most blatant of sins or of any one type of sin, either. To transgress the law at any point is to be full of guilt. Don't try to cover up your sins as some say David did. That only highlights the fact that there is sin there.

While I am bitter with my King and his actions, I am also more aware of the fact that I too am a sinner in need of God's forgiveness. Perhaps I need to learn to forgive so God may forgive me.

But for now, I am only aware of my faults. Of the faults of my people. Of the sin of all people everywhere.

Even you.

David's sin is your sin. Your sin is my sin. We are all covered in the muck and the mire.

All we can do now is rely upon God to lift us out of the mud.

CARAVANNER

Imagine my surprise when I arrived in the city.

I had driven past on numerous occasions. I had noted the empty buildings and ruined walls that had surrounded the city. I had tried to imagine where the roads had been, where the markets had been, where the Temple had been. At times it was all clear to me; at other times it was an impossibility. No one could live here.

How many times had our caravan stopped nearby? I don't know. 30? 40? We stayed in the ruined city only once. It was an eerie place. We almost felt the anguish of the people who had died in their attempt to protect their way of life. But they were no more. Life was over for them.

And the few who had survived had been taken away to a foreign land many thousands of miles away.

In Babylon I once talked to a man who had seen the destruction of Jerusalem. He wept as he spoke. He told me of the glory he had known which I could hardly imagine. I had seen the aftermath. That could not have been as wonderful as he described it.

But this past trip through the land of Israel proved me wrong!

I came down the valley as usual when I noticed that the once barren hilltop was no longer barren. There was a city wall that followed the ridge line — and buildings inside the wall!

Fortunately we were ahead of schedule, so I talked the head driver into a rest so I could find out what was going on.

I found the wall was complete but that the gates were not finished. People and animals were still free to come and go at will. It would not be long before this would be a strong fortress — as strong as in the days of King David when no one dared attack.

Once inside, I wandered around to where a large crowd of people had gathered. I had never seen a single person in this area, and now there was easily a crowd of 10,000 people. It was clear that they were intent on listening to a group of people who were on a raised platform, a stage, if you will, where everyone could see. At the edge of the crowd you could barely tell that someone was talking. His words were too faint to hear.

So I began to ask about the city wall, about the people, and about the one who was speaking.

There was excitement in the air that was clearly echoed in the voices and mannerisms of those who told me their story. Clearly what they were talking about was no less of a miracle than when the walls of Jericho fell when Joshua led their ancestors into this land a thousand years earlier.

It seems that a man called Nehemiah was primarily responsible. He recognized the implications of their exile, had a vision of a resettlement, and now they were celebrating the fulfillment of God's promises.

Nehemiah had been in the King's Court in Babylon when he heard the stories of people like myself. He grieved for the culture and city that had died with the destruction of Jerusalem. His people had no more identity. And he saw the implications for his children. His remorse and sadness came to the attention of the King who offered to remedy the situation.

But that was not enough, they told me. Ezra had been given a similar promise, but it didn't go anywhere.

Nehemiah had a vision. He knew what was needed.

His vision was of a rebuilt city. His vision was of a re-inhabited city. His vision was of a renewed community that would worship and live according to the law of Moses.

The vision of Nehemiah was going to take time and effort to realize, so he enlisted the help of anyone who claimed to be of Jewish heritage. This meant that people who would later be called Samaritans were accepted in the labor force as well as descendants of Levi and Aaron who maintained a more pure ancestral heritage were needed to continue in the faith of Abraham and Isaac and Israel.

Nehemiah kept his vision alive by rehearsing it in the presence of the workers who worked on the walls around the city. When trouble arose he insisted that building the wall was of primary importance; bearing arms to protect against would-be attackers was only secondary.

"God will provide," Nehemiah had told them. "God will protect us." "Our task is to build."

And build they did. They were getting tired of it, too. The stones were heavy. Food was difficult to obtain. And their bodies were getting weary.

Nehemiah then called for Ezra to come. The wall was almost complete. The Temple was already in use, but the people needed to stop and remember why they were working so hard, why they were here, what the vision of Nehemiah was all about.

And so they rested in the seventh month to celebrate.

Now, most of the people who were working were Jews, but none of them had honored the annual feasts and festivals in their entire life. They had only heard about them from their parents and grandparents.

The seventh month was a time to remember how their ancestors had lived in the wilderness, how they had struggled for survival for forty years, and how God had brought them safely to a new land, the land "flowing with milk and honey." It was a time to celebrate what God had been doing in their land in their lives.

What better time to celebrate the rebuilding of the city walls?!

Ezra read the story of God's revelation to Moses and the promises fulfilled in those days and of the immense joy as the people looked and saw the things around them. There were buildings where there had only been brush. There were people where only animals had lived.

This was indeed a new day! This was the beginning of a new civilization in accord with the promises of God!

And this was a celebration! Food, drink, song, and dance.

On the way home, I spent hours and hours in reflection.

What I had seen was no normal celebration. This was indeed a miracle. And yet, I couldn't help but think that there was more.

You see, I began to recognize a loss in my own life, too. I no longer took time to seek God or even to pray. I had gone to spending my free time in sin. I ate too much. I drank too much. I found comfort outside the love of God.

The temple within me was in ruins. I was in moral decay. There was nothing left. I was in need of a rebuilding. I had exiled God and it was high time to change.

I began identifying God's vision for me and my life. I began to find ways to let God settle within me. I needed a resettlement to take place.

O, the city of my heart is not yet rebuilt, but it *is* now under construction. And I am finding immense joy in my new-found faith. I am finding reasons to celebrate, and I am continually singing a song of joy to God who has re-inhabited my soul.

Someday, the temple of my soul will be complete. Until then, I sing songs of praise and continue to make room for God in my life.

BARTHOLOMEW

Earlier this week I heard a child ask her mother, "When do we eat?" and in hearing that question I was reminded of an incident that happened some time ago. I remember it like it was yesterday.

Philip and I were just returning from Capernaum to find Jesus. He had sent us out to the villages to teach and to preach and to bring healing to the people (Mk. 6:7-9). When we found him, James and John had just finished telling about their trip and Peter and Andrew were just starting to tell their tales. As usual, Andrew had to continually correct Peter as he told Jesus all about the events of the last few days.

Philip and I had just started when Thomas and Matthew arrived. We told Jesus about the child who had a fever that went away when we anointed her with oil. We reported that many people had heard a message very much like ours from John the Baptist, and many were very receptive to making a change in their lives. We didn't know exactly how many, but we estimated there were over 200 people who repented!

By the time we finished telling our story, James and Thaddeus and Simon and Judas had arrived — and a whole crowd had gathered around us. Peter interrupted Jesus before he started to take reports from the other six and asked Jesus when we were going to eat.

I couldn't believe it! Sure, we hadn't had much to eat over the last few days, but there were more important things to be doing right now!

But as always, Jesus was more compassionate than I was. He saw the need to get away and rest and to break bread together; so we got into a boat and headed to one of our favorite coves to rest and relax (Mk. 6:31-32). As we started out, Jesus took the time to hear the other reports and began to teach us.

Have you ever heard Jesus tell a story? He's fantastic! I could sit and listen to him all day long! He knows how to make the stories come alive!

On the boat, he told us the story of Elijah. He told us how our people had turned from God; how they began to rely on their military might to maintain control of the land and how they no longer listened to the prophets; how they began to worship the Canaanite God, Baal. At about that time, Jesus told us, God called Elijah to go before the people with a message. The message was to prove who was the most powerful God in the land and who was the only God to be worshipped. God stopped the clouds (1 Kgs. 17:1). No more rain or dew for three long years.

In the midst of this terrible drought, however, God made a promise to meet Elijah's needs. First, he was sent to a cool brook and a raven came and brought him morsels of bread and meat (1 Kgs. 17:6). It doesn't sound like much, but it was enough for Elijah to survive on — at least until the brook dried up. Then God sent Elijah to a widow and her son. Elijah found her gathering sticks for their last meal; but she willingly shared that meal with Elijah (1 Kgs. 17:12-14). And God blessed her for giving out of her lack — God ensured that the jar of meal never went empty and that the cruse of oil never ran dry. And Elijah, the woman, and her son survived the drought.

About the time Jesus told us that, we arrived in our cove. But to our surprise, to our dismay, a crowd was waiting for us there (Mk. 6:33)! Couldn't we ever get a few minutes alone, I thought?

But Jesus reminded us of another story. Moses was concerned about our people going into the Promised Land without a leader. He had been up on the mountain talking with God when he saw the crowd meandering around. His image of what it looked like was the same one that Jesus used to describe this crowd on the hillside: they look like sheep without a shepherd (Nu. 27:16-17). Having said that, Jesus got out of the boat and began to teach the people.

While we tied up the boat, Peter turned to Andrew and asked him why Jesus had told us the story of Elijah. Was he suggesting that there was going to be another drought in the land? We discussed it for some time. The common consensus was that Jesus was trying to make Peter see that when we are doing God's will, we don't need to ask, "When do we eat?" We will be taken care of.

It seemed to fit in with what Jesus had said before, when he gave us the sermon from the mount. I don't remember the exact words, but it was something about seeking God's kingdom first and that all of our needs would then be provided for (Mt. 6:33). I do remember the illustration he used was that of the lilies of the field that never worry about things and yet they continue to bloom and seem to be the best dressed creatures of the land (Mt. 6:28-29).

We pretty much decided that Jesus had given us this message today in response to Peter's anxieties about eating. So when we finished tying up the boat, we joined the crowd on the hillside.

Jesus was teaching with stories and parables, like he usually did, and I was fascinated with the ideas he was bringing before us. I almost forgot the time — until I heard the man's stomach next to me growl. I realized it was getting late, and if we didn't send these people home soon, they wouldn't have enough strength to make the trip. During the next break I shared my concern with Jesus (Mk. 6:35-36).

His response really caught me unprepared! He told me to *feed* them (Mk. 6:37)! I tried to explain that we didn't have enough money to feed 5,000 people, and that even if we did, by the time we went into town, bought some food, and brought it back, it would be dark, and the people will have gone home without anything.

But he was serious. He told me again to feed them. He asked me how much food I had (Mk. 6:38). I didn't have any, but I checked with the others, and between the twelve of us, we found five loaves and two fish. I reminded Jesus that that meant there was one loaf for every thousand people here, and that this would never be enough.

But he took the bread, gave thanks for it, gave it to us and told us to pass it out among the people (Mk. 6:41). It was then that I noticed the crowd was sitting in rows and that our job would be fairly easy. After we passed out the bread and fish, we returned to Jesus, not knowing what to expect next. He told us to gather up the crumbs! (I thought for sure he had lost his mind; there couldn't be anything left over.) But we each took a basket and began to collect the crumbs. What amazed me was not that I had a full basket when I finished, but that everyone I talked to said they had had enough to eat (Mk. 6:42)!

A miracle had taken place right before my eyes! After we gathered the crumbs, Jesus told us to get into the boat and head back. He wanted to say a few more things and would follow us. In the boat, we all began to talk about what had happened. No one could quite believe it. Peter said that it was like the widow who fed Elijah. She shared what little she had, and God multiplied it for her. We shared what little we had, and God also multiplied it for us.

Thomas wouldn't accept that. He never believed anything. He said that what had happened was that we shared what little we had, which inspired others in the crowd to share what little they had. The miracle was that generosity had rubbed off on the others there. This seemed to make sense, but no one wanted to believe it.

Then Thaddeus said something that has lived with me ever since. He said that it reminded him of the manna in the wilderness. The people had been complaining, and God heard their concern and provided food for them (Ex. 16:3-4). It wasn't much, but it was enough. But the most important part of the manna story was that God provided the food so they would know who God was and that God was concerned about them. They had not been deserted — and neither had we. And in Deuteronomy, it says the manna was given to the people so that they would know that we don't live by bread as much as we live by God's word (Dt. 8:3). Our sustenance really comes from God.

That made the most sense to me. We were witnesses to a miracle where God had showed loved and compassion for us, and it was done in the context of Jesus' teaching. What we had heard from him was what provided our sustenance, not the bread. And everyone was satisfied.

When I heard that little girl ask her mother, "When do we eat?" I wondered if she knew it didn't really matter, because we don't live by food, but by the very word of God!

Thanks be to God.

Amen.

ISAAC

My name is Yitzhak. I suppose you would say my name is "Isaac," but that's because you speak English and I, well, I speak Aramaic and Hebrew — and Greek, too. And in Hebrew my name is יצהק

But I don't want to talk about my name. I want to tell you about someone who changed my life and the day I met him.

I am a scribe. I have been a scribe since I was old enough to recite the Torah — when I had my bar mitzvah. (That was when I turned twelve years old and was welcomed as an adult into the Jewish community.)

O, I remember that day well. I was asked to read from the Torah and then to make a comment about my reading. In many ways, it was like the countless bar mitzvah's I've been to before and since my own; but it was my own, so I remember it differently.

I remember, for instance, the reading that day was when Moses was expounding upon the Great Commandments. He said,

Qatsar qatsiyr 'erets kalah pe'ah sadeh . . .

Oh yeah, I forgot that you don't speak Hebrew. Let me read it to you in English:

> When you reap the harvest of your land, you
> shall not reap to the very edges of your field,

or gather the gleanings of your harvest. You shall not strip your vineyard bare, or gather the fallen grapes of your vineyard; you shall leave them for the poor and the alien: I am the LORD your God.

You shall not steal; you shall not deal falsely; and you shall not lie to one another. And you shall not swear falsely by my name, profaning the name of your God: I am the LORD.

You shall not defraud your neighbor; you shall not steal; and you shall not keep for yourself the wages of a laborer until morning. You shall not revile the deaf or put a stumbling block before the blind; you shall fear your God: I am the LORD.

You shall not render an unjust judgment; you shall not be partial to the poor or defer to the great: with justice you shall judge your neighbor. You shall not go around as a slanderer among your people, and you shall not profit by the blood of your neighbor: I am the LORD.

You shall not hate in your heart anyone of your kin; you shall reprove your neighbor, or you will incur guilt yourself. You shall not take vengeance or bear a grudge against any of your people, but you shall love your neighbor as yourself: I am the LORD.

You shall keep my statutes. You shall not let your animals breed with a different kind; you shall not sow your field with two kinds of seed; nor shall you put on a garment made of two different materials. — Lev. 19:9-19

Can you imagine what it must have been like for me? I read that passage — in Hebrew — and then I had to tell people what I thought it was about . . . oy vey!

In trying to figure it out, I concluded that God intends for us to live our lives differently than those who live around us. Not because we are special. Not because we are better than other people. We are to live differently because God is special, because God is superior to all other gods, because God is different.

Your word 'holy' tries to capture what that means — to be different, to be special, to be set apart.

We are called by Moses to be a holy people (Lev. 19:2). I understand that as Christians you are also called to be a holy people in your scriptures (see 1 Pet. 1:15-16, for instance); in fact, as Methodists, you are taught to work towards perfection! My, what an awesome goal!

My own bar mitzvah was the first time I was allowed to speak to people about the Torah. And I knew the particular lesson I was given was a sign from God about how I was to live my life. It wasn't just about the people who were there that day; it was about me, it was about my life.

So I began to study the Torah faithfully and carefully. I made a choice then to follow as much of the Law of Moses as I could. It was then that I became a scribe.

Of course that meant I learned to recite the entire Torah almost from memory. And I became an avid student of the scriptures. I've spent most of my waking hours since that day reading the Torah and learning about it.

You know, in our system of education, we are taught to ask questions, to challenge one another and to test one another. One of my assignments early on was to number the various laws and commands and rules. I wasn't the first one who had to do it, of course, and I know lots of others who have done it since.

But I was intrigued by the answer I found — and I began to ask my own questions.

- Why are there 613 laws?
- Is it possible to keep all 613 of them?
- If you keep 612 of them, are you still living a life that is different from the world around you?
- What if you only keep 607? Or 512? Or 19?
- Is there one law that you must keep to still be considered a faithful Jew?

Of course there have been as many answers to my questions as there have been people to ask. And I still keep asking.

In the meantime, I try to live up to all 613 commands. I don't often interpret the law for others, but I do try to obey it. That's what makes me a scribe — though I like to think that's what makes me a faithful Jew.

There are others who are good at interpreting the law or arguing about the subtleties of the law — even though they are not as interested in keeping the law. Some of these people have even formed schools around their particular interpretations.

In my day, there were three major 'schools' of thought regarding the law. There were Pharisees, Sadducees, and Essenes. I would often enter into discussions with them, but was typically frustrated by the way they worked out their theories without a sincere effort to practice them.

But still, my favorite times were the festivals in Jerusalem when all kinds of people would gather on street corners and discuss the law. I was always trying to learn more about it while trying to live up to it.

That's where I came into contact with the man who changed my life.

Some Pharisees and then some Sadducees had been raising their questions to him, but it was pretty obvious that they weren't interested in his answers. It was almost like they were trying to trick him into saying something he would regret.

But I was really impressed with him. He had not only thought through his ideas, he obviously knew how to live according to his understanding of the law, creating a sense of harmony in his life that was hard to refute.

I liked that about him. He was honest and had integrity. So when I got a chance, I asked him my questions.

- What laws are essential?
- What are the most important ones?
- Is there one law in particular that if we kept it faithfully we could still consider ourselves to be faithful Jews?

His answer sounded like an alarm going off in my head. He quoted the very law that I had read at my bar mitzvah! Surely this was a sign from God!

Only he put it alongside another law, making it take on a whole new dimension. He said,

> 'Hear, O Israel: the Lord our God, the Lord is one; you shall love the Lord your God with all your heart, and with all your soul, and with all your mind, and with all your strength.' The second is this, 'You shall love

your neighbor as yourself.' There is no other commandment greater than these" — Mark 12:29-31.

Certainly, if one of the Pharisees had said it that way I would have discounted it — after all, they didn't know how to love God **or** their neighbor. All they knew how to do was talk **about** God and their neighbor.

The answer Jesus gave me seemed so pure and so true; and it was also clear that he knew how to genuinely love both God and his neighbor.

I knew it was the right answer. And for knowing he was right, he assured me that I wasn't far from the Kingdom of God.

But I also knew I was far, far away. I knew that I could not fully live up to the demands he put before me even though in my study and in my learning and in my living, I had become very adept at obedience.

The problem was I had forgotten how to love.

Ever since that day, I've been trying to figure out what it means to love. I'm not sure I'll ever understand what love is.

But then, maybe that's my problem. Maybe I keep trying to study love without doing it . . . like the Pharisees did with the law.

Could I stay and watch you? I've heard that you all know how to love. Maybe I can learn by watching you.

Maybe you can teach me what love is.

SOSTHENES

What God can do is almost too amazing to explain. The power of God's grace to transform lives is simply amazing. Take my story, for instance.

When Paul came to Corinth, I was the Vice President of the synagogue. I'm not sure what the equivalent position would be in your church. In the synagogue, that's the person who does all the work, makes none of the decisions, and is only noticed when something goes wrong.

If you've never had that official title, maybe you can remember a time when that's how it felt.

But don't get me wrong. Crispus, the President of the synagogue was a good man. It's just the way the synagogue was organized. The President always led the meetings. It didn't matter who the President was, he decided who would speak each week. He also decided when to have dinners. He made all of the decisions.

And whenever there was work to be done, he turned to the Vice President, who made sure the work was done. The Vice President found lodging for guests, for instance. He not only prepared the room for meetings and dinners, he would stand in the background to ensure that everyone had everything they needed — everything from chairs to plates to wine.

And if anything ever went wrong, the President would always turn to the Vice President.

Well, Crispus had invited Paul to preach. So I had to find him a place to stay, a place to eat, and a place to prepare his message. When he was invited back the third time, I asked Justus if Paul could stay with him since he lived next door to the synagogue. It looked like it might go on for some time, and his house was the natural first choice for a long-term guest of the synagogue.

But that only seemed to make things worse. Crispus and maybe half of the congregation all became Christians in response to what Paul had been saying. The remaining members of the synagogue turned to me and insisted that I *do* something about it. When I explained that I was only the Vice President, they evicted Crispus and elected me President.

And the next time the Roman proconsul came through Corinth, they insisted that I bring Paul and the other Christians to the Roman court. But Gallio didn't want to hear our case — and the Jews took it out on *me*! I was beaten and thrown out of the synagogue along with the Christians — all because I had made it so easy for Paul to win converts to the faith.

But you probably knew all about that.

Forgive me. I didn't mean to bore you by repeating that part of the story.

The amazing revelation of God's grace is what I wanted to tell you about. For me, it came when I was trying to figure out how to make the best of the circumstances. I was a Jew who was no longer welcome in the synagogue. So I turned to the only other place I knew I could find Jews like me — I turned to the church.

It seemed a little strange at first, but they used familiar scriptures. The people made me feel quite welcome, too. I had known many of them from the synagogue, but even the ones I didn't know seemed to welcome me as if I were family to them.

Some of them had been Christians before they came to Corinth. Some had become converts to the faith after hearing a different preacher, a man named Apollos. One man had been a part of our synagogue years earlier. He told the story of going to Jerusalem for the Festival of Weeks and being there when Peter first preached to the people. He talked about Pentecost in a way few others could because he was there!

And while I felt welcome in the church, it was also different from any other synagogue I'd ever attended. Like many Jewish congregations, there were transients who were traveling through as well as local residents. But there were also Gentile converts — adding a dimension to worship I'd never thought possible. It was a reminder to me that our God — the God of Abraham, Isaac, and Jacob — was also the God of all people.

But that was only part of the revelation I found.

As I said, I was struggling with how this faith — this story of Jesus — could help me in my dilemma. First it was Crispus, the former synagogue President, and then Aquila, a man who came to Corinth as a Christian, and then Paul himself, who told me the story of how Jesus had also been an innocent victim who suffered for doing what was right. Jesus had been stripped and beaten — just like I had been. But he had also been crucified, even though, like me, he had done nothing wrong.

They explained that in response to what Jesus had done, they were simply telling his story — the miraculous story of how God righted the wrong by raising Jesus from the dead and offering him new life — a gift they now claimed as a promise for their lives as well.

Week after week, I heard story after story of people who were willing to give their lives, to share their livelihood, to carry the burdens of one another. They didn't try to change my mind about Jesus or even to punish me for being who I was. They simply told me what had happened in their lives and in the lives of others. They let me watch as they lived their lives in response to this amazing story of Jesus.

They helped me see the truth that had always been there. As much as I thought I understood about the scriptures before, their stories were like an unveiling of sorts, a revealing of who God had always been.

And when I came to see the truth of the story of Jesus — I don't know how to explain it — it was like I was given my own new life. They reminded me that my own name, Sosthenes, meant "of safe strength." They recognized gifts God had given me, things I didn't even know about myself. They saw how I was a good listener who had the strength to make others feel safe when they spoke.

And then through my open ears, others eventually saw an unveiling of God's grace, too. Christ himself was being revealed in the church — revealed in the lives of people like Paul and Crispus and even me!

It was years later when I would find myself at Paul's side as he wrote a letter to that same church, the one that saw how God was at work in me. He asked for my insights into their current situation because I had lived in Corinth longer and had been there more recently than he had been.

I used the gifts I had been given to help Paul get an accurate picture of their situation. It's funny because in many ways it was like being the Vice President of the synagogue again. He was making all of the decisions; he was deciding what to say, while I was providing all of the background information.

Only this time I knew that God was at work. It was an unveiling of something that they had allowed to become hidden again.

And what I heard in his letter was as much for me as it was for them.

You see, God is still working on me. The story of Jesus, the offer of new life he gave is only the beginning point in my "new" life. It's my desire to allow God to make me completely holy so that *everything* I do will reveal Christ.

It doesn't always happen, but whenever it does, I give thanks to God for allowing me to be his servant. It's amazing what God is able to do!

HORN OF OIL

Some have compared me to Aladdin's lamp, for I have been around for many, many years. And within me there are stories of wonder, stories of power, stories of glory, stories of death, and stories of destruction. I was crafted in Midian, by a nice man named Jethro.

At the marriage feast of his daughter, Zipporah, Jethro made a feast out of an old ram. It was an old ram, but the way he cooked the meat it was the most delightful anyone had ever tasted. And during the week-long marriage celebration, Jethro carefully and skillfully carved out of one horn a flask, a vial, which he filled with the most expensive perfume he could find. It was his final gift to the new couple, a horn of oil.

I know this was true because, I am that vial.

Moses treated me with the utmost respect. I never left his side. My oil had been used to treat the cuts and abrasions Moses received as well as those of his sheep. He had me with him when he first heard God speak in the burning bush. He had me with him when he crossed the Red Sea. He had me with him when he received the commandments from God on Mt. Sinai.

But I was most proud of the part I played in setting his brother Aaron apart. Moses took some of that precious oil and poured it on Aaron as a sign of him being chosen by God to serve as priest (Ex. 29:7).

I remember how Aaron knelt down in the middle of all the elders. Moses poured oil on his head and it flowed down his beard and onto his shoulders and chest. He was never the same, nor were the people who witnessed it.

Everyone knew I had been in the presence of God. The scent of the perfume became a reminder to all of the invisible yet powerful presence of God in their midst. I became the vehicle through which people were to offer prayers to God. Prayers of hope, prayers of anguish, prayers for strength and prayers for guidance.

I became a powerful symbol in their lives.

And while Moses passed his mantle on to Joshua, he left me with Aaron's son, Eleazar (Num. 4:16). At his side, I accompanied him each year into the Holy of Holies. I was there for every sacrifice. I was there for every celebration of importance.

I witnessed the fall of the walls at Jericho and I was there when the first child was born in the promised land. My oil was a healing balm to the ill and a powerful reminder of God's guidance and leadership during the times of the Judges.

That's when I learned that being emptied was my important task. If I was only a storage vessel, there was no power to be seen. There was no fragrance to smell.

I continued to be used by priest after priest until the time of Eli. He became afraid of my oil. He feared the people wouldn't know what to do if God began to act and bring healing. So he kept my oil within me.

Those were sad times. I knew God was present, but my oil never filled the rooms with fragrance and people began to forget. I was left behind at times and forgotten.

Even after Eli died and Samuel became recognized as one who spoke to God and to whom God spoke, I was often left behind.

Not until God told Samuel to take me and anoint a king was I brought out into public again.

Those were my glory years.

Everyone recognized me. Samuel began to carry me with pride and purpose. He brought me first to a man named Saul (1 Sam. 10:1). Saul was a striking man. He stood over six feet tall and could see over the heads of all the people of Israel.

When Samuel poured oil from me that day, Saul bent way down low. The humility of Saul made the fragrance even more pleasing to God. And my oil became associated with the power and presence of God's spirit once again. Saul became King and everyone rejoiced.

But Samuel kept me by his side. And every time he visited the King, I was there. Samuel seemed to use me to remind Saul how he became King. It wasn't because of who he was, but because of who God was. It was my oil that made him King. And Samuel made it a point to remind him of God's will, God's desire, and God's judgment.

Especially when Saul wanted to ignore God. Samuel asked him, have you forgotten what the oil smells like? He opened me up and let him be reminded.

Did you know that in the human mind, the sensory interpretation for smells is very close to the place where memories are stored?

To smell my oil again brought Saul's mind back to the day he had bent his neck and submitted to the yoke of God, to the times when he emptied himself so that God could be seen.

But he forgot too often and too soon.

You see, the fact that God chose him didn't make him right. He had to continue listening to God. Each and every day he had to choose to follow God's call. And he began not to choose to do so more and more often. He turned his back on God and forgot his own anointing.

So God told Samuel to take me again and anoint another king. We saw several people that I thought would be perfect kings. Like Saul, they were tall. Like Saul, they were smart. Like Saul, they were willing to bow down and accept God's call in their lives.

But God had someone else in mind.

At first I was a little stunned. A little boy. No more than eleven or twelve. And while he was cute with his red hair and fair complexion, I couldn't help but wonder if he'd remember my oil any better than Saul had.

Boy was I surprised! This boy who became King, this shepherd who became a leader, was also a poet and singer.

He even sang songs about me!

You probably know one of them: "Thou anointest my head with oil" he sang (Ps 23:5). He sang that song until the last days of his life. He did remember me. And he asked to see me and smell my ointment often — at least once a year, he asked the priest to anoint him again.

I was very present. I was very visible. And my presence kept everyone's mind on God, the God I represented, the God whose presence was even more durable than mine.

David continued to seek God's will and to do God's will. He understood that just because he had been chosen didn't mean God could be ignored. He was God's servant, God wasn't his servant. And I served to remind him of that fact. That in emptying himself, God was allowed to fill him up.

But after Zadok used me to anoint Solomon, I was put on the shelf again. Only used when a new king came along. I became part of a ritual rather than a vibrant symbol of the presence of God. And my oil became stale.

But I wasn't always forgotten.

Prophets like Isaiah, spoke wistfully of a day when someone would be anointed again, anointed in such a way that my presence would be welcomed, anointed in such a way that God's spirit would be recognized, anointed in such a way that the fragrant spices would fill the nostrils of the King and the priests and the prophets and the people.

I became lost before that ever took place.

Hidden away in a cave. Forgotten by the hoards of people who have come and gone. Ignored by those who most needed to smell my oil and sense God's presence in their midst.

But even without me, people can still be called by God. People like you have been called by God. People have been anointed for one purpose or another. Some of you have been anointed, and you know it. Not always anointed with oil, but anointed, none the less.

Of course, you must choose how to respond to God's call. God simply invites you to be a partner in ministry. God lets you make the decisions along the way.

There is one who came who was anointed by God in a very special way, though not with the oil in me. He, like David, was not what people were expecting. And the oil of his anointing came from a rather unusual place, though there was a tale in ancient Israel that seems to speak about it:

The trees once went out
  to anoint a king over themselves.
So they said to the olive tree,
  'Reign over us.'
The olive tree answered them,
  'Shall I stop producing my rich oil
    by which gods and mortals are honored,
    and go to sway over the trees?'
Then the trees said to the fig tree,
  'You come and reign over us.'
But the fig tree answered them,
  'Shall I stop producing my sweetness
    and my delicious fruit,
    and go to sway over the trees?'
Then the trees said to the vine,
  'You come and reign over us.'
But the vine said to them,
  'Shall I stop producing my wine
    that cheers gods and mortals,
    and go to sway over the trees?'
So all the trees said to the bramble,
  'You come and reign over us.'
And the bramble said to the trees,
  'If in good faith you are anointing me king
over you,
    then come and take refuge in my shade;
but if not, let fire come out of the bramble
    and devour the cedars of Lebanon.'
                                    — Judges 9:8-15

Anointed in the shade of thorns, not the sweet smell
of scented oil. How sad that I was lost. How tragic that
I was not used. No oil anointed Jesus until the time
of his death. But it was his crown of thorns that both

indicted the people and invited the people to accept him as the anointed King.

But, how glorious that he humbly accepted the call.

The real question, however, is how have you responded to God's call? How have you emptied yourself so that God's power can be experienced through your life?

I have been lost and forgotten for a long time. But God still anoints people with oil. God anoints people like you. And you have the choice of emptying yourself in response or ignoring God's call.

What will you do?

CPSIA information can be obtained
at www.ICGtesting.com
Printed in the USA
BVHW082119090323
660081BV00001B/230